DREAMS

Unlocking The Prophetic
Language of the Night

TOM CORNELL

Dreams

Unlocking the Prophetic Language of the Night

Tom Cornell

SOZO PUBLISHING

Paperback ISBN: 978-1-969882-01-2

Bible quotations are taken from:

Contents

Introduction

The Power of Dreams, The Midnight Messenger

It was a restless night, and I found myself caught in the tension between sleep and wakefulness. As I drifted into slumber, I suddenly found myself standing in a vast open field, a gentle breeze moving through golden wheat stalks. A figure, clothed in radiant white, approached me. Though His face was shrouded in light, His voice carried the weight of eternity.

"WRITE DOWN WHAT YOU SEE," HE SAID.

I looked down and saw a scroll in my hands, words appearing on it as if an unseen hand was inscribing them. The letters were not in a language I knew, yet somehow, I understood their meaning deep within my spirit. As I awoke, the presence of God still lingered in my room. I knew—without question—that I had just received a dream from the Lord.

Dreams are more than fleeting images or the byproducts of an overactive mind; they are divine messages from the throne room of heaven. Scripture is filled with stories of men and women who received divine revelation in their sleep—Joseph, Daniel, Solomon, and even the Pharaoh of Egypt. From Genesis to Revelation, God has consistently used dreams to communicate His purposes, warn of impending danger, impart wisdom, and reveal His will. And He is still speaking today.

But how do we recognize when a dream is from God? How do we interpret what He is saying? And most importantly, how do we respond to these midnight messages?

The Biblical Foundation of Dreams as Divine Communication

Throughout history, God has chosen to reveal His will through dreams. In the Book of Job, we find a striking passage that confirms this reality:

"For God may speak in one way, or in another, yet man does not perceive it. In a dream, in a vision of the night, when deep sleep falls upon men, while slumbering on their beds, then He opens the ears of men, and seals their instruction." (Job 33:14-16 NKJV)

This passage suggests that dreams are not accidental; they are intentional. God seals instruction within them, embedding divine wisdom and revelation into the fabric of our subconscious.

The Bible records over 200 references to dreams and visions, reinforcing their significance in the ways God communicates with His people. In Genesis, God used dreams to reveal the destiny of Joseph, a young man whom He would raise to rule Egypt (Genesis 37:5-10). In the New Testament, an angel appeared to Joseph, the earthly father of Jesus, in a dream, warning him to flee to Egypt for the safety of the Messiah (Matthew 2:13).

One of the most profound affirmations of dreams as divine communication is found in the prophecy of Joel 2:28 NKJV, which was reiterated by the Apostle Peter on the Day of Pentecost:

"And it shall come to pass afterward that I will pour out My Spirit on all flesh; your sons and your daughters shall prophesy, your old men shall dream dreams, your young men shall see visions."

This was not just a statement about a distant future—it is the reality of the New Covenant Church. We are living in a prophetic age where the Holy Spirit is actively speaking to His people through dreams, and those who are sensitive to His voice can unlock hidden wisdom and divine direction.

Why Does God Speak in Dreams?

Many wonder why God chooses to speak through dreams when He could simply give direct instructions in waking life. The answer lies in the way God has designed us.

Dreams bypass human reasoning.

When we are awake, our logical mind often filters out the voice of God, dismissing supernatural impressions as mere thoughts. However, in sleep, our spirits are more receptive because our analytical mind is at rest.

Dreams engage the heart.

God often speaks in symbols, metaphors, and parables, just as Jesus did during His earthly ministry. Why? Because images and narratives have a profound impact on the heart. A dream can bypass resistance and communicate deep truths that might otherwise be rejected in waking moments.

Dreams invite us into deeper intimacy.

When God speaks in a dream, He often does so in a way that requires pursuit. Dreams are an invitation to dialogue with the Lord, to seek His wisdom and understanding. They draw us into a place of deeper reliance on the Holy Spirit for interpretation.

Understanding the Language of the Spirit in the Night

Dreams often come in symbolic form, much like the visions given to the prophets of old. God speaks in a divine language that requires discernment and wisdom to decode. Jesus Himself frequently spoke in parables, using stories to reveal the mysteries of the Kingdom. Likewise, dreams operate on a similar principle. Instead of giving direct statements, God often uses imagery, numbers, colors, and emotions to communicate His message.

Take, for example, Nebuchadnezzar's dream in Daniel 2. He saw a massive statue made of different metals—gold, silver, bronze, iron, and clay. This dream was not merely a collection of strange images; it was a detailed prophecy about the future kingdoms of the world. Daniel, through divine wisdom, was able to interpret its meaning, demonstrating that dreams require both revelation and interpretation.

The Apostle Paul wrote in 1 Corinthians 2:14 that

"the natural man does not receive the things of the Spirit of God, for they are foolishness to him; nor can he know them, because they are spiritually discerned."

In other words, dreams must be interpreted spiritually, not intellectually. The Holy Spirit is the only One who can unlock the mysteries of dreams and visions.

The Role of the Holy Spirit in Dream Interpretation

Many people make the mistake of relying on human reasoning or dream dictionaries to interpret what they see at night. While there are common symbols in the language of dreams, no interpretation is complete without the guidance of the Holy Spirit.

Just as Joseph and Daniel depended on God to interpret dreams, we too must develop a relationship with the Holy Spirit, allowing Him to be our Teacher. John 16:13 NKJV tells us:

"However, when He, the Spirit of truth, has come, He will guide you into all truth; for He will not speak on His own authority, but whatever He hears He will speak; and He will tell you things to come."

The Holy Spirit is our divine interpreter. He not only

reveals the meaning of dreams but also shows us how to respond. Dreams are not just informational—they are invitations to action.

If we receive a warning dream, it may call us to intercession. If we receive a directional dream, it may require obedience. If we receive a revelatory dream, it may be for a later time. This is why we must cultivate a lifestyle of dream stewardship—writing down our dreams, seeking the Lord in prayer, and learning to recognize His voice in the night.

The Call to Dream Again

We are living in days where God is awakening His people to the supernatural realm. Dreams are not just for biblical times; they are for today. If you have ever dismissed your dreams as insignificant, I encourage you to take another look. Ask the Holy Spirit to give you eyes to see and ears to hear. Begin to journal your dreams and seek Him for their meaning.

The same God who spoke to Joseph, Daniel, and Solomon is speaking to you. Will you listen?

Chapter 1

The Biblical Pattern of Dreams
God's Language in the Night

IT WAS WELL PAST MIDNIGHT WHEN THE ANCIENT KING was stirred from his sleep. Nebuchadnezzar, ruler of Babylon, had been given a dream so troubling that he called for all his wise men, demanding an interpretation. But there was a problem—he had forgotten the dream itself. Panic filled the palace as the astrologers and magicians admitted they had no ability to retrieve or interpret what was lost in his subconscious. Then came Daniel, a man of prophetic insight, who sought God in prayer and received both the dream and its meaning.

What happened in that royal court was more than just an impressive act of divine revelation; it was a confirmation that God has always spoken through dreams and still does today. The God of Abraham, Isaac, and Jacob—the God of Daniel, Joseph, and Paul—is the same yesterday, today, and forever. He has not stopped using dreams as a means of divine communication.

Dreams have been a consistent thread throughout biblical

history, serving as a prophetic language in every era. They are not merely subconscious musings or symbolic riddles; they are invitations from the divine realm, a means by which God reveals His plans, warnings, and guidance to His people.

To understand the significance of dreams in the life of the believer, we must first examine how God has used dreams throughout Scripture.

How God Used Dreams in the Bible

From Genesis to Revelation, dreams played a vital role in the unfolding of God's divine plan. They were not random or meaningless occurrences but strategic moments where heaven invaded the affairs of men.

Dreams in the Old Testament

The first recorded dream in the Bible occurs in Genesis 20, when God speaks to Abimelech in a dream, warning him not to take Sarah as his wife. This moment establishes a foundational truth: dreams can serve as divine warnings to protect individuals from sin or danger. But perhaps one of the most well-known examples of divine dreams is the story of Joseph, the son of Jacob.

- Joseph's Dreams (Genesis 37:5-10) – Joseph, as a young man, receives prophetic dreams foretelling his rise to leadership. Though misunderstood and ridiculed by his family, his dreams ultimately come to pass when he becomes second-in-command over Egypt. His story teaches us that dreams can reveal our destiny, but they may require years of preparation and trials before fulfillment.

- Pharaoh's Dreams (Genesis 41:1-32) – Years later, Pharaoh receives troubling dreams of seven fat cows being devoured by seven thin cows, followed by seven healthy heads of grain consumed by withered ones. None of his advisors can interpret the dream, but Joseph, through divine revelation, reveals its meaning: seven years of plenty followed by seven years of famine. This encounter demonstrates how dreams can provide insight into future events and prepare us for what is to come.

- Jacob's Dream (Genesis 28:10-17) – As Jacob flees from his brother Esau, he falls asleep and sees a vision of a ladder stretching between heaven and earth, with angels ascending and descending. God reaffirms His covenant with Jacob, marking this as a significant moment of divine encounter through dreams.

- Solomon's Dream (1 Kings 3:5-15) – Solomon, in a dream, receives the offer from God to request whatever he desires. Instead of asking for wealth or power, he asks for wisdom. This dream illustrates that God can grant divine impartation and revelation through the night season.

- Daniel's Interpretation of Nebuchadnezzar's Dream (Daniel 2:1-49) – King Nebuchadnezzar receives a troubling dream, and Daniel is the only one who, through God's wisdom, can both recall and interpret it. This affirms that dreams often contain prophetic revelation concerning nations and world events.

Dreams in the New Testament

While some assume that dreams were only prevalent in the Old Testament, the New Testament continues this pattern, reinforcing that God still speaks through dreams under the New Covenant.

- Joseph, the Earthly Father of Jesus (Matthew 1:20-24; 2:13,19,22) – In a series of dreams, Joseph receives instructions concerning Mary's pregnancy, warnings about Herod's plot, and direction to relocate his family. His dreams confirm that God gives supernatural guidance through dreams, especially in critical moments of decision.
- Pilate's Wife (Matthew 27:19) – On the day of Jesus' trial, Pilate's wife has a disturbing dream warning her husband not to have any part in condemning Jesus. This demonstrates how God can send warning dreams even to those outside the covenant community.
- Paul's Macedonian Vision (Acts 16:9-10) – Paul, in a night vision (a form of a dream), sees a man from Macedonia pleading for help. This dream directs his missionary journey, illustrating that dreams can serve as divine assignments, revealing where God wants us to go.
- John's Revelatory Visions (Book of Revelation) – The entire Book of Revelation is based on the visions given to John while he was in the Spirit. Though technically a vision rather than a traditional dream, it affirms that God uses the language of the night to reveal heavenly realities.

The Continuity of Dreams in the Modern Church

Some argue that dreams were unique to biblical times, yet Scripture gives no indication that God has ceased speaking through them. In Joel 2:28 NKJV, God declares:

"And it shall come to pass afterward that I will pour out My Spirit on all flesh; your sons and your daughters shall prophesy, your old men shall dream dreams, your young men shall see visions."

This prophecy was confirmed in Acts 2:17, when Peter stood on the Day of Pentecost and proclaimed that what was happening was a fulfillment of Joel's prophecy. This means that dreams are a function of the outpouring of the Holy Spirit and will continue as long as the Spirit is moving in the earth.

Countless believers today can testify to supernatural dreams that have provided guidance, warnings, encouragement, and prophetic insight. From church leaders to everyday individuals, people are encountering God in the night, just as He spoke to Joseph, Daniel, and Paul.

Recognizing the Biblical Pattern

Dreams are not an outdated or mystical concept—they are a primary way God communicates with His people.

- God has used dreams throughout Scripture to reveal His plans, give warnings, provide guidance, and affirm His covenant.
- Both the Old and New Testaments affirm the role

of dreams, proving their continuity in God's
dealings with humanity.

- The outpouring of the Holy Spirit ensures that
  dreams remain a part of the prophetic life of the
  Church today.

If God spoke through dreams then, He still speaks through dreams now. The question is not if He is speaking—the question is, are we listening?

Chapter 2

The Three Sources of Dreams
Discerning the Voice Behind the Dream

It was around 3 a.m. when Sarah woke up in a cold sweat. She had just experienced an unsettling dream—one where she was walking through a dark forest, pursued by an unseen presence. The fear clung to her even after she awoke. Confused and disturbed, she wondered, Was this from God?

That same night, halfway across the world, a pastor in Africa had a different experience. In his dream, an angel appeared to him, instructing him to prepare his church for a coming season of revival. He woke up feeling the presence of the Lord so strongly that he immediately fell to his knees in prayer.

Two people. Two dreams. Two very different sources. Not every dream is from God. In fact, dreams originate from one of three primary sources:

Divine Dreams – Dreams that come from God for guidance, warning, or revelation.

Soul Dreams – Dreams that arise from our emotions, thoughts, or subconscious processing.
Demonic Dreams – Dreams that originate from the enemy, bringing fear, confusion, or deception.

The ability to discern the source of a dream is essential for proper interpretation. Many believers either dismiss all dreams as meaningless or assume that every dream is a divine message. Both perspectives are dangerous. Instead, we must develop spiritual discernment, allowing the Holy Spirit to reveal the true origin and purpose of our dreams.

Divine Dreams – Messages from God
The Purpose of God-Given Dreams

Dreams from God serve specific functions. They are not random, nor are they self-serving. When God gives a dream, it has one or more of the following purposes:

- Guidance – Directing someone toward a particular decision or path.
- Warning – Revealing danger or hidden threats.
- Encouragement – Strengthening someone's faith and hope.
- Revelation – Unveiling hidden truths or prophetic insight.
- Intercession – Calling someone to pray over a person or situation.

Throughout Scripture, we see God using dreams to accomplish these divine purposes.

Biblical Examples of Divine Dreams:

- Joseph's Dream (Matthew 1:20-24) – An angel appeared to Joseph, reassuring him that Mary's pregnancy was divine and instructing him to take her as his wife.
- Paul's Macedonian Vision (Acts 16:9-10) – Paul received a night vision (a form of a dream) calling him to bring the gospel to Macedonia.
- Pharaoh's Dream (Genesis 41:1-32) – God warned Pharaoh of a coming famine, leading Joseph to prepare Egypt for what was ahead.

These examples confirm that when a dream is from God, it will align with His character, His Word, and His purposes. Divine dreams do not contradict Scripture or promote confusion—they illuminate God's will and lead to righteousness.

How to Recognize a Divine Dream

A dream may be from God if:

- It brings peace, even if it contains a warning.
- It aligns with Scripture.
- It carries a sense of divine weight and importance.
- It leaves you with an urgency to pray, act, or seek confirmation.
- It leads to spiritual growth or a deeper connection with God.

However, not all dreams carry this divine imprint. Some originate from within us, reflecting our emotions, anxieties, or desires.

Soul Dreams – The Subconscious at Work
What Are Soul Dreams?

Soul dreams come from our own minds, emotions, and subconscious processing. They are neither from God nor from the enemy, but rather a reflection of our internal world.

For example:

- A person dealing with anxiety may dream of being chased or trapped.
- Someone longing for a relationship may dream of being with a particular person.
- A person working on an important project may dream about it repeatedly.

These dreams are natural and often influenced by:

- Personal experiences (past trauma, current stress, or joyful moments).
- Emotional state (fear, excitement, insecurity, or desire).
- Daily activities (movies, books, conversations, and thoughts before bed).

Biblical Example of a Soul Dream:

Ecclesiastes 5:3 says, "For a dream comes through much activity, and a fool's voice is known by his many words." This passage suggests that some dreams are simply the result of an active mind processing daily events.

For instance, if someone watches a thrilling action movie

before bed, they may have intense dreams that night. This doesn't mean the dream is prophetic—it simply reflects what their mind absorbed that day.

How to Recognize a Soul Dream

A dream is likely from the soul if:

- It is repetitive but lacks divine weight.
- It reflects personal concerns rather than spiritual revelation.
- It is influenced by recent activities, emotions, or media consumption.
- It lacks a strong sense of urgency or divine instruction.

While soul dreams may not carry spiritual revelation, they can still be valuable. Sometimes, they reveal areas where we need healing, deliverance, or deeper trust in God.

Demonic Dreams – Counterfeits and Deceptions
What Are Demonic Dreams?

Just as God speaks through dreams, the enemy can also use dreams as a weapon. These dreams are designed to:

- Instill fear – Creating nightmares that torment the soul.
- Deceive and manipulate – Leading people into false beliefs or sinful behavior.
- Oppress and attack – Bringing confusion, lust, or demonic encounters.

- Distract from God's purposes – Turning attention away from the Holy Spirit.

Demonic dreams can include nightmares, sexual dreams, or encounters with dark entities. These are not just psychological experiences—they can be spiritual attacks designed to open doors to oppression.

Biblical Examples of Demonic Influence in Dreams

- False Dreams and Deception (Jeremiah 23:25-27) – God warned about false prophets who claimed to receive dreams but were leading people astray.
- Dreams that Cause Fear (Job 4:12-15) – Eliphaz describes a terrifying dream where a spirit passed before his face, bringing fear and dread.
- Satanic Influence in Dreams (Matthew 13:25) – Jesus spoke of the enemy sowing tares while men slept, symbolizing how the enemy works in the unseen realm.

How to Recognize a Demonic Dream

A dream may be from the enemy if:

- It brings intense fear, oppression, or confusion.
- It promotes sin, temptation, or ungodly desires.
- It feels spiritually heavy or dark.
- It contradicts the character of God and His Word.

Not every scary dream is demonic, but if a dream leaves a

lasting sense of fear, darkness, or oppression, it's wise to rebuke it and pray for protection.

How to Discern the Source of a Dream

When you wake up from a dream, ask yourself:

1. <u>What was the primary feeling in the dream?</u>

   - Peace and clarity? → Likely from God.
   - Confusion or fear? → Could be from the enemy.
   - Anxiety or randomness? → Likely from the soul.

2. <u>Does the dream align with Scripture?</u>

   - If yes → It may be divine.
   - If no → It could be deception.

3. <u>What is the fruit of the dream?</u>

   - Does it bring you closer to God or away from Him?
   - Does it lead to repentance, prayer, and wisdom?

Jesus said, "You will know them by their fruits." (Matthew 7:16). The same principle applies to dreams—the fruit will reveal the source.

Learning to Discern

God is speaking in dreams, but so is the enemy, and so is the human soul. Not every dream is prophetic, but every dream has a source.

- Divine Dreams come from God and lead to spiritual growth.
- Soul Dreams reflect personal thoughts and emotions.
- Demonic Dreams attempt to deceive, tempt, or bring fear.

The more we walk closely with the Holy Spirit, the easier it becomes to discern the voice behind the dream. Are you paying attention to the voice of the night?

Chapter 3

The Purposes of Prophetic Dreams
Why Does God Speak Through Dreams?

Throughout history, God has chosen to communicate with His people in different ways—through His written Word, through prophets, through angelic visitations, and through the still, small voice of the Holy Spirit. But one of the most consistent and mysterious ways He speaks is through dreams.

Dreams are more than just symbolic images or random subconscious thoughts; they are intentional messages from heaven, sent to guide, warn, encourage, and prepare us for what is to come. Every dream has a purpose, but not every dream serves the same purpose. In this chapter, we will explore five primary purposes of prophetic dreams:

1. **Warning Dreams** – God's way of protecting us from danger.
2. **Directional Dreams** – Giving us instruction on where to go or what to do.

3. **Encouragement Dreams** – Strengthening our faith and hope.
4. **Calling and Destiny Dreams** – Revealing God's purpose for our lives.
5. **Intercessory Dreams** – Assigning us to pray for people or situations.

Understanding these purposes will help us respond correctly to the dreams we receive, stewarding them in a way that aligns with God's will.

Warning Dreams – *Divine Alerts from Heaven*

God often uses dreams to warn His people of coming danger. These dreams serve as divine alerts, allowing us to pray, prepare, or change course before something harmful happens.

<u>Biblical Example: Joseph Warned to Flee</u>

One of the clearest examples of a warning dream is found in Matthew 2:13 (NKJV). After the birth of Jesus, Joseph received a dream in which an angel warned him:

"Arise, take the young Child and His mother, flee to Egypt, and stay there until I bring you word; for Herod will seek the young Child to destroy Him."

Because of this dream, Joseph immediately took Mary and Jesus and fled to Egypt, saving the Messiah from Herod's massacre.

Signs of a Warning Dream

- There is an urgent sense of danger.
- The dream may involve threats, disasters, or an enemy's attack.
- It carries a clear call to action—flee, pray, or prepare.

How to Respond to a Warning Dream

1. Pray immediately – Ask God for wisdom on how to respond.
2. Seek confirmation – If needed, ask a mature believer to help discern the dream's meaning.
3. Act in obedience – If the dream calls for action, do not delay.

Many times, God gives warning dreams to intercessors so they can pray against demonic plans before they unfold.

Directional Dreams – *God's GPS for Your Life*

Some dreams are meant to provide divine direction—to tell us where to go, what to do, or how to proceed in a given situation.

Biblical Example: Paul's Macedonian Dream

In Acts 16:9-10 (NKJV), the Apostle Paul received a dream in which a man from Macedonia pleaded with him, saying:

"Come over to Macedonia and help us!"

Paul recognized this as divine instruction. He immediately changed his course, traveling to Macedonia to preach the gospel. This decision led to the planting of the first church in Europe.

Signs of a Directional Dream

- A specific place, person, or task is highlighted.
- The dream brings a strong sense of clarity and purpose.
- It leads to kingdom advancement or obedience to God's will.

How to Respond to a Directional Dream

1. Write it down – Document every detail of the dream.
2. Pray for confirmation – Directional dreams should be tested through prayer.
3. Obey in faith – If the dream aligns with God's Word and is confirmed, take action.

Many life-altering decisions have been made because of a single dream from God.

Encouragement Dreams – *Strengthening Our Faith*

God knows when we are weary, discouraged, or in need of reassurance. Sometimes, He gives dreams that bring encouragement, peace, and renewed faith.

Biblical Example: Jacob's Ladder

In Genesis 28:10-17, Jacob was running for his life, alone and uncertain about his future. One night, he had a dream in which he saw a ladder extending from earth to heaven, with angels ascending and descending. In the dream, God reaffirmed His covenant with Jacob, saying:

"I am with you and will keep you wherever you go."
When Jacob awoke, he declared:
"Surely the Lord is in this place, and I did not know it!"

Signs of an Encouragement Dream

- It brings a deep sense of peace and hope.
- It reminds you of God's faithfulness and presence.
- It strengthens your spirit to keep moving forward.

How to Respond to an Encouragement Dream

1. Thank God for His word of encouragement.
2. Use the dream to strengthen your faith.
3. Share the dream if it is meant to uplift others.

Encouragement dreams often come in seasons of difficulty when God wants to remind us that He is near.

Calling and Destiny Dreams – *Revealing God's Plans for Your Life*

Some dreams contain glimpses of our future—the assignments, ministries, and purposes that God has prepared for us.

Biblical Example: Joseph's Prophetic Dreams

In Genesis 37, Joseph had two dreams that foretold his future leadership. In the first, his brothers' sheaves of wheat bowed to his. In the second, the sun, moon, and eleven stars bowed before him. Though he did not fully understand them at the time, these dreams revealed his destiny as a ruler. Many years later, Joseph became second-in-command in Egypt, saving his family and an entire nation from famine.

Signs of a Calling or Destiny Dream

- It reveals something about your future.
- It often involves symbols of authority, influence, or leadership.
- It may take years to fully unfold.

How to Respond to a Calling Dream

1. Pray for wisdom and patience.
2. Do not rush the process—God's timing is key.
3. Stay faithful in small things while waiting for the promise.

Many people receive calling dreams but struggle with impatience. Just as Joseph had to endure trials before stepping into his destiny, we too must allow God to refine us before we step into our calling.

Intercessory Dreams – *The Call to Prayer*

Some dreams are not about us, but about others. In these dreams, God gives us prayer assignments—to intercede for individuals, churches, or even nations.

Biblical Example: King Nebuchadnezzar's Dream

In Daniel 2, Nebuchadnezzar had a dream that disturbed him, but he did not understand its meaning. God gave Daniel the interpretation, revealing that the dream was prophetic insight into world history. This shows that some dreams require intercession and revelation to be understood.

Signs of an Intercessory Dream

- The dream involves a person, city, or nation you may not personally know.
- It carries a burden to pray.
- It often includes symbols of urgency or warfare.

How to Respond to an Intercessory Dream

1. Pray immediately for the person or situation.
2. If appropriate, share the dream with those involved.
3. Continue praying until God gives release.

God gives intercessory dreams to those willing to pray. They are not always about personal benefit but about partnering with heaven's agenda.

The Right Response to a Prophetic Dream

Dreams are not given just for information—they are given for action. Whether a dream brings a warning, direction, encouragement, a calling, or an intercessory assignment, it demands a response. Are you paying attention to what God is speaking in the night?

Chapter 4

The Symbolic Nature of Dreams
Why Does God Speak in Symbols?

IF GOD WANTED TO COMMUNICATE SOMETHING important to you, wouldn't it be easier for Him to simply say it plainly? Why would He use symbols, metaphors, or parables instead of straightforward instructions? The answer lies in the nature of God and His desire for relationship and revelation.

Throughout Scripture, God has always used symbolic language to communicate spiritual truths. Jesus Himself often spoke in parables, and when His disciples asked why, He replied:

"To you it has been given to know the mysteries of the kingdom of heaven, but to them it has not been given... Therefore, I speak to them in parables, because seeing they do not see, and hearing they do not hear, nor do they understand." (Matthew 13:11,13 NKJV)

God veils truth in symbols for several reasons:

- Symbols engage the heart, not just the mind. –
  They require spiritual discernment and
  relationship with the Holy Spirit.
- Symbols invite us to seek revelation. – They
  encourage prayer, study, and deeper intimacy with
  God rather than relying on quick answers.
- Symbols protect truth from the enemy. – Certain
  revelations are reserved for those who diligently
  seek God.

Dreams are often parabolic in nature—meaning they are stories, images, and metaphors that require interpretation. God does this not to confuse us but to invite us into a journey of revelation.

The Role of Personal and Cultural Symbolism in Dreams

One of the biggest mistakes people make in dream interpretation is assuming that every symbol has a universal meaning. While many symbols do have biblical significance, God can also use personal and cultural symbols unique to an individual.

Biblical Symbolism

Many symbols in Scripture carry consistent meanings. For example:

- Water → Can represent the Holy Spirit (John
  7:38) or cleansing.
- Fire → Often symbolizes purification or the
  presence of God (Exodus 3:2).

- Snakes → Frequently represent deception or demonic influence (Genesis 3:1).
- Bread → Can symbolize the Word of God (Matthew 4:4) or communion (John 6:35).

When interpreting a dream, comparing symbols with Scripture is crucial. However, while biblical symbolism provides a foundation, not all dream symbols are directly found in the Bible.

Personal Symbolism

God often speaks personally to each individual, using symbols that have specific meaning based on their life experiences. For example:

- Someone who was raised near the ocean may dream of the sea as a place of peace.
- Another person, who nearly drowned as a child, may dream of the sea as a place of fear or danger.
- A musician may have dreams involving musical instruments, which could symbolize worship, creativity, or calling.

God uses what is familiar to you to speak in ways you will understand. This is why dream interpretation is not just about looking up symbols in a dictionary—it requires seeking God for revelation.

Cultural Symbolism

Different cultures ascribe various meanings to symbols. For instance:

- In some cultures, an owl represents wisdom.
- In others, an owl may be a symbol of death or bad omens.
- In Western culture, a white dress typically represents purity.
- In some Asian cultures, white is associated with mourning.

Understanding cultural context is important because God speaks to people in ways they can relate to.

Common Dream Symbols in Scripture

While not every dream symbol has a universal meaning, there are many recurring symbols in the Bible that give us a foundation for interpretation.

1. Water

- Still, clear water → Peace, the Holy Spirit, refreshing (Psalm 23:2).
- Stormy or muddy water → Confusion, spiritual warfare (Isaiah 57:20).
- A flood → Overwhelming circumstances or judgment (Genesis 6:17).

2. Fire

- God's presence (Exodus 3:2 – the burning bush).
- Purification (Malachi 3:2-3 – refining fire).
- Judgment (Hebrews 12:29 – "Our God is a consuming fire").

3. Trees

- A fruitful tree → Spiritual growth, prosperity (Psalm 1:3).
- A withered tree → A warning of spiritual decline (Matthew 21:19).
- A tree cut down → Judgment or a season ending (Daniel 4:14).

4. Roads and Paths

- A straight road → Walking in God's will (Proverbs 3:6).
- A fork in the road → A choice that needs to be made.
- A narrow path → The way of righteousness (Matthew 7:14).

5. Animals

- Dove → The Holy Spirit, peace (Matthew 3:16).
- Lion → Jesus as the Lion of Judah (Revelation 5:5) or the enemy (1 Peter 5:8).
- Serpent → Satan, deception (Genesis 3:1).
- Sheep → God's people (John 10:27).

6. Numbers in Dreams

Numbers often have symbolic meaning in Scripture:

- 1 → Unity, new beginnings.
- 3 → The Trinity, divine completeness.
- 7 → Perfection, completion.

- 12 → Government, apostolic authority.
- 40 → A time of testing or transition.

Numbers in dreams should be interpreted within their context.

How to Discern the Meaning of Symbols in Your Dreams

Since dreams are highly symbolic, the key to interpretation is discernment. Here are practical steps to understand what God is saying through symbols:

1. Write the Dream Down Immediately

- Capture as many details as possible.
- Include colors, emotions, locations, and actions.

2. Identify Key Symbols

- Ask, What stands out most in the dream?
- List the objects, colors, numbers, and emotions present.

3. Compare with Scripture

- See if the symbol has biblical significance.
- Look for patterns in how the Bible uses that image.

4. Consider Personal and Cultural Meaning

- Ask, What does this symbol mean to me personally?

- Consider if it has any specific significance in your life.

5. Seek the Holy Spirit's Revelation

- Pray and ask God to reveal the dream's meaning.
- Not every symbol is literal—some represent spiritual truths.

6. Look for Patterns Over Time

- If the same symbols keep appearing in your dreams, God may be establishing a personal dream language with you.
- Patterns in dreams often reveal themes God is emphasizing in your life.

Avoiding Common Pitfalls in Dream Interpretation

1. Avoid Legalistic or Formulaic Thinking

Dream interpretation is not a mechanical process—it is a spiritual journey of discovery. Two people could see the same symbol but have different meanings based on their lives and context.

2. Do Not Rely Solely on Dream Dictionaries

While lists of biblical symbols can be helpful, they are not a substitute for the Holy Spirit's guidance. Avoid the trap of thinking every dream can be solved like a puzzle—dreams are about relationship, not formulas.

3. Do Not Assume Every Dream is from God

As we covered in the previous chapter, some dreams are from the soul or the enemy. Always test dreams through Scripture and the peace of the Holy Spirit.

Unlocking the Language of the Spirit

God speaks in symbols because He wants us to seek Him for understanding. Rather than just giving quick answers, He draws us into deeper intimacy by requiring us to engage with Him in interpreting dreams.

Are you willing to go beyond surface-level understanding and seek God's wisdom in the mysteries of the night?

Chapter 5

Biblical Dream Symbols and Their Meanings

Unlocking the Symbols of the Spirit

Have you ever woken up from a dream filled with strange imagery—running water, a soaring eagle, a house with many rooms—and wondered, What does this mean?

God speaks through symbols and imagery, much like He did throughout Scripture. However, biblical dream interpretation is not about formulas or one-size-fits-all definitions. Instead, it requires spiritual discernment, prayer, and the guidance of the Holy Spirit.

In this chapter, we will explore some of the most common symbols found in biblical dreams, along with their possible meanings. While this list is not exhaustive, it provides a foundation for understanding how God uses objects, colors, numbers, and people to communicate His divine messages.

Let's dive into the language of dreams and begin unlocking the prophetic imagery of the night.

Elements of Nature in Dreams

Water

Water often represents the Holy Spirit, purification, or spiritual renewal. However, the condition of the water matters.

- Still, clear water → Peace, spiritual refreshing (Psalm 23:2).
- Rivers or flowing water → The move of the Holy Spirit (John 7:38).
- Stormy or muddy water → Confusion, spiritual warfare (Isaiah 57:20).
- A flood → Overwhelming circumstances or divine judgment (Genesis 6:17).

Fire

Fire can signify God's presence, purification, or judgment.

- A burning bush → Divine calling (Exodus 3:2).
- Refining fire → God's process of purifying a person (Malachi 3:3).
- Destructive fire → Judgment or demonic attack (Hebrews 12:29).

Wind

Wind often represents the Holy Spirit or divine movement.

- A gentle breeze → God's presence (1 Kings 19:12).
- A mighty rushing wind → The Holy Spirit's power (Acts 2:2).

- A destructive storm → Spiritual warfare or shaking (Job 1:19).

Mountains
Mountains symbolize high places, obstacles, or divine encounters.

- Standing on a mountain → Spiritual authority or revelation (Exodus 19:20).
- Climbing a mountain → Seeking God or spiritual elevation (Psalm 24:3).
- A mountain in the way → An obstacle that must be overcome (Mark 11:23).

Trees
Trees often represent people, nations, or spiritual life.

- A flourishing tree → Righteousness and spiritual growth (Psalm 1:3).
- A barren tree → Lack of fruitfulness or judgment (Matthew 21:19).
- A tree being cut down → The end of a season or judgment (Daniel 4:14).

Common Objects in Dreams

Houses
A house in a dream often represents a person's life, a family, or a spiritual dwelling place.

- A well-kept house → Spiritual stability and growth.

- A broken-down house → Spiritual neglect or generational struggles.
- A house with many rooms → Expanding into new spiritual capacities (John 14:2).

Doors and Gates
Doors and gates symbolize opportunities, transitions, or spiritual access.

- An open door → A new opportunity or divine invitation (Revelation 3:8).
- A closed or locked door → A season of waiting or a missed opportunity.
- A gate → A place of authority or access (Matthew 16:19).

Bridges and Roads
Bridges and roads often represent life's journey and spiritual paths.

- A straight road → Walking in God's will (Proverbs 3:6).
- A fork in the road → A decision that needs to be made.
- A narrow path → The way of righteousness (Matthew 7:14).

Vehicles (Cars, Trains, Planes, Boats)
Vehicles often represent ministries, callings, or spiritual assignments.

- Driving a car → A personal journey or leadership role.

- Riding in a bus or train → A corporate or church movement.
- Flying in a plane → A higher spiritual calling or breakthrough.
- A sinking boat → A crisis of faith or spiritual attack (Matthew 8:23-27).

Animals in Dreams

Positive Animals

- Dove → The Holy Spirit, peace (Matthew 3:16).
- Eagle → Spiritual vision, prophetic calling (Isaiah 40:31).
- Lamb → Jesus, innocence, sacrifice (John 1:29).
- Lion → Jesus as the Lion of Judah or spiritual authority (Revelation 5:5).

Negative Animals

- Serpent → Satan, deception (Genesis 3:1).
- Wolf → False teachers, spiritual danger (Matthew 7:15).
- Scorpion → Demonic attacks (Luke 10:19).
- Dog → Carnal desires or unclean spirits (Philippians 3:2).

Colors in Dreams

Colors in dreams often carry symbolic significance:

- White → Purity, righteousness, holiness.
- Red → The blood of Jesus, sacrifice, war.

- Blue → Revelation, the Holy Spirit, heavenly realms.
- Green → Growth, prosperity, new life.
- Gold → Divine glory, kingship, refinement.
- Black → Mystery, sin, hidden things, judgment.

Numbers in Dreams

Numbers often have prophetic meaning in Scripture:

- 1 → Unity, new beginnings.
- 3 → The Trinity, divine completeness.
- 7 → Perfection, completion.
- 12 → Government, apostolic authority.
- 40 → A time of testing or transition.

For example, if you repeatedly dream about the number 7, God may be confirming completion in an area of your life.

People in Dreams – Literal or Symbolic?

People in dreams may represent:

1. Themselves (literal meaning).
2. A characteristic or spiritual influence.
3. A role or calling (pastor, teacher, prophet).

For example:

- Seeing a pastor may represent spiritual leadership.
- A father figure could symbolize God the Father or authority.

- A child could represent innocence, new beginnings, or immaturity.

Always discern whether the person is literal or symbolic by praying for interpretation.

How to Interpret Dream Symbols Correctly

1. Seek the Holy Spirit First
Never assume that a symbol has only one meaning—ask God what He is saying through it.

2. Look at the Context of the Dream
The setting, emotions, and interactions in the dream help determine what the symbol means in that specific dream.

3. Compare Symbols with Scripture
Does the symbol align with biblical meanings, or does it have a different personal meaning for you?

4. Record and Pray Over Recurring Symbols
If a symbol keeps appearing in your dreams, God may be highlighting something specific in your life.

Learning the Language of Heaven

Dreams are not just random images—they are messages filled with divine meaning. However, symbols require discernment, and the best interpreter is the Holy Spirit Himself.

Are you willing to learn the language of dreams and seek God's wisdom in unlocking their meaning?

Chapter 6

The Importance of Context in Dream Interpretation

Why Context Matters in Dream Interpretation

IMAGINE RECEIVING A LETTER WRITTEN ENTIRELY IN symbols. A dove, a mountain, a river, and a house appear on the page. Without context, you might recognize the symbols but completely misunderstand their meaning.

This is how many people approach dream interpretation. They focus on individual symbols while missing the bigger picture of the dream's message. A dream is like a puzzle, and the context is what helps put the pieces together correctly. Context in dream interpretation includes:

1. The Emotional Tone of the Dream – How did you feel in the dream?
2. The Setting of the Dream – Where did the dream take place?
3. The Key Objects and Actions – What was happening, and what symbols stood out?
4. The People in the Dream – Are they literal or symbolic?

5. Your Personal Life and Spiritual Season – How does the dream relate to your current situation?

Dreams are not just static images; they are dynamic experiences where every emotion, action, and setting contributes to the meaning. If we misinterpret the context, we risk misunderstanding what God is saying.

The Emotional Tone of the Dream

One of the first questions you should ask when interpreting a dream is: How did I feel during the dream? Emotions in dreams often reveal the spiritual atmosphere and can indicate whether the dream is:

- From God (peace, revelation, joy, urgency).
- From your soul (stress, confusion, personal desires).
- From the enemy (fear, oppression, despair).

Examples of Emotional Context in Dreams

- A dream of flying with a feeling of freedom → Could represent a spiritual breakthrough.
- A dream of being chased but feeling overwhelming terror → Could indicate a spiritual attack or an area where fear is controlling you.
- A dream of standing in a large house and feeling joyful → Could symbolize entering a season of blessing and expansion.

The same dream symbols can mean different things depending on the emotional context.

<u>Example:</u>

- Seeing a lion in a dream while feeling peace →
  Could represent Jesus as the Lion of Judah.
- Seeing a lion while feeling afraid and under attack
  → Could represent the enemy, who prowls like a
  lion (1 Peter 5:8).

<u>Steps to Discern Emotional Context</u>

1. Write down your emotions immediately upon
   waking.
2. Ask the Holy Spirit to confirm if the emotion was
   from Him.
3. Compare it with Scripture—does it align with
   God's character?

The Setting of the Dream

The location of a dream provides clues about its meaning.
Where did the dream take place?

- A church → Could symbolize spiritual matters or
  your role in the Body of Christ.
- A school → Could represent a season of learning or
  spiritual growth.
- A battlefield → Could indicate spiritual warfare.
- A house → Could represent your personal life or a
  generational issue.

<u>Example:</u>

- A dream of being in an old childhood home could mean God is revealing something about your past or childhood wounds that need healing.
- A dream of walking through a city filled with lights could symbolize entering a season of influence or expansion in your calling.

Questions to Ask About the Setting:

1. Is this place familiar or unfamiliar?
2. Does this location represent something significant in my life?
3. How do I feel about this place?

The spiritual atmosphere of the setting matters. A bright, peaceful place often represents God's presence, while a dark or chaotic place may represent confusion, danger, or spiritual warfare.

The Key Objects and Actions in the Dream

What objects or actions stood out the most in the dream? Actions in dreams often reveal what God is saying about your current spiritual walk.

Examples of Actions and Their Possible Meanings

- Climbing a mountain → Overcoming obstacles, seeking God's presence.
- Crossing a river → Transition, moving into a new spiritual season.
- Being given a key → Receiving spiritual authority or revelation.

- Running but not moving → Feeling stuck in your calling or spiritual life.
- Writing in a book → A call to steward revelation, a prophetic calling.

Objects in dreams also carry symbolic significance.

<u>Example: Seeing a Door in a Dream</u>

- An open door → A new opportunity or calling.
- A locked door → A season of waiting or a barrier that needs to be overcome.
- A revolving door → Going in circles, repeated patterns in life.

<u>How to Analyze the Actions in a Dream:</u>

1. Identify the main action—what were you doing?
2. Consider whether the action was effortless or difficult—was there struggle or ease?
3. Compare it with your current season of life—does it relate to something happening now?

The People in the Dream – Literal or Symbolic?

People in dreams can represent:

- Themselves (literal meaning).
- A characteristic or spiritual influence.
- A role or calling (pastor, teacher, prophet).

<u>For example:</u>

- Seeing a pastor may represent spiritual leadership.
- A father figure could symbolize God the Father or authority.
- A child could represent innocence, new beginnings, or immaturity.

<u>Are They Literal or Symbolic?</u>

To discern if a person is literal or symbolic, ask:

1. Do I know this person personally? If so, is God highlighting them for intercession?
2. What role does this person play in my life? If it's a teacher, they might represent learning. If it's a leader, they might symbolize spiritual authority.
3. Does this person remind me of someone else? God sometimes uses someone familiar to symbolize another person in your life.

<u>Example:</u>

- A dream of a friend handing you a gift could mean that God is using them to bring you encouragement or revelation.
- A dream of a stranger warning you could represent an angelic messenger.

How Your Personal Life and Spiritual Season Affect Dream Meanings

Dreams are not always about the future—sometimes they reveal what is happening now. Ask yourself:

1. Is this dream related to something I am currently going through?
2. Does this confirm something God has already been speaking to me?
3. Am I in a season of transition, warfare, waiting, or breakthrough?

<u>Example:</u>

- If you are about to step into a leadership role, and you dream of standing on a mountain, God may be preparing you for the responsibility ahead.
- If you are struggling with fear, and you dream of being trapped in a dark room, God may be revealing a stronghold that needs to be broken.

<u>Responding to a Dream Based on Your Spiritual Season</u>

1. Pray for confirmation – Ask God if this dream is speaking to your current situation.
2. Seek wise counsel – A mature believer may help discern what God is revealing.
3. Journal your dreams over time – Patterns may emerge that provide deeper understanding.

Context is the Key to Understanding

Symbols alone do not reveal the full meaning of a dream—context is the key. The emotional tone, setting, actions, people, and your current spiritual season all play a role in dream interpretation. Before seeking an answer, always ask: "What is the full context of this dream?"

Dreams are a divine invitation to seek deeper understanding. Are you willing to go beyond surface-level interpretation and pursue the heart of God in your dreams?

Chapter 7

Dreams and Their Connection to Prophetic Destiny

God Speaks Through Dreams to Reveal Destiny

IMAGINE STANDING AT A CROSSROADS IN LIFE, UNSURE OF the path ahead. You've been praying for guidance, but no clear answer comes—until one night, you have a vivid dream. In it, you see yourself stepping onto a stage, speaking to thousands, or perhaps standing in a foreign land, ministering to people you've never met before. You wake up with an unshakable sense that God just revealed something about your future.

Dreams have long been a vehicle for divine direction, offering glimpses of God's calling and purpose for our lives. Throughout Scripture, God used dreams to reveal assignments, confirm callings, and align people with His plans. In this chapter, we will explore how God uses dreams to:

1. Reveal a person's calling and destiny.
2. Confirm prophetic words and divine assignments.
3. Provide direction and preparation for the future.
4. Show us our place in His kingdom purposes

Your dream life is not random—it is an ongoing conversation with heaven about the things you are called to accomplish on earth.

1. Dreams That Reveal Calling and Destiny

Some of the most powerful biblical dreams were given to reveal destiny.

<u>Joseph's Dreams – A Prophetic Glimpse of His Future.</u>
Joseph was a young man when he had two prophetic dreams about his future role as a leader.

"Then Joseph had a dream, and when he told it to his brothers, they hated him even more. He said to them, 'Please listen to this dream which I have had: We were binding sheaves in the field, and behold, my sheaf stood up and also remained standing, and behold, your sheaves gathered around and bowed down to my sheaf.'" (Genesis 37:5-7 NKJV)

In a second dream, the sun, moon, and eleven stars bowed before him. While his family misunderstood his dreams, they were a prophetic preview of his calling to rule in Egypt.

However, Joseph's dream was not fulfilled immediately. In fact, his journey toward destiny included betrayal, imprisonment, and years of waiting. Yet, every challenge he faced was preparing him to step into his God-ordained purpose.

<u>Daniel's Night Visions – A Call to Influence Nations</u>
Daniel, a captive in Babylon, received prophetic dreams and night visions that revealed both his

personal destiny and the future of entire empires (Daniel 7-12). His ability to interpret dreams positioned him as an advisor to kings, fulfilling a unique calling to influence political and spiritual realms.

This teaches us that God doesn't just give destiny dreams to pastors or prophets—He also calls people into government, business, and other spheres of influence through dreams.

2. Dreams That Confirm Prophetic Words and Assignments

God often uses dreams to confirm what He has already spoken through prophecy, Scripture, or divine encounters.

Paul's Macedonian Call – A Dream That Confirmed His Next Mission
In Acts 16:9-10 (NKJV), Paul received a directional dream that confirmed his next assignment.

"During the night, Paul had a vision of a man from Macedonia, standing and pleading with him, saying, 'Come over to Macedonia and help us.' When Paul had seen the vision, we immediately sought to leave for Macedonia, concluding that God had called us to preach the gospel to them."

This dream was a divine confirmation of where Paul needed to go. He obeyed the dream and carried the gospel into new territory, shaping the course of church history.

Gideon's Enemy Has a Prophetic Dream
In Judges 7:13-15, Gideon overhears an enemy soldier recounting a dream about a barley loaf rolling into their

camp and destroying their tents. Another soldier correctly interprets the dream, realizing it symbolizes Gideon's victory.

What's amazing about this story is that God used a dream to confirm Gideon's calling—even through his enemies! This teaches us that sometimes our destiny is revealed through dreams given to others as well.

3. Dreams That Prepare Us for the Future

God not only reveals destiny through dreams—He also prepares us for what is coming.

Pharaoh's Dream of Famine – Preparation Through Prophetic Dreams

Pharaoh had two dreams about seven years of plenty followed by seven years of famine (Genesis 41). While Pharaoh himself did not understand them, Joseph interpreted the dreams and provided a strategy to save Egypt from disaster.

This shows us that God doesn't just reveal what is coming He also provides wisdom for how to prepare.

Jesus Warns Peter About His Future in a Dream-Like Encounter

In Luke 22:31-32 (NKJV), Jesus tells Peter:

"Simon, Simon, Satan has asked to sift you like wheat. But I have prayed for you, that your faith may not fail. And when you have turned back, strengthen your brothers."

While not a traditional dream, this prophetic word prepared Peter for a coming test. Later, when Peter denied Jesus, he remembered the word and repented—ultimately stepping into his destiny as a leader in the early church.

God will sometimes give warning dreams that prepare us for hardships or transitions. If we ignore these dreams, we might miss the opportunity to respond correctly before challenges arise.

4. Dreams That Reveal Our Role in God's Kingdom

Not all destiny dreams are personal—some reveal our role in a much larger plan.

<u>John's Visions of the Future Church</u>
The entire book of Revelation is based on John's night visions and prophetic dreams. Through these revelations, God revealed the destiny of the Church and the end-time plan for humanity.

This shows us that some dreams are meant to give us a kingdom perspective—revealing how we fit into God's global and eternal purposes.

<u>Modern-Day Destiny Dreams</u>
Even today, God is calling people into their destinies through dreams.

- A young woman dreams of helping orphaned children—later, she starts a ministry rescuing trafficked kids.

- A businessman dreams of building a financial foundation for kingdom work—years later, he funds churches and missionaries worldwide.
- A worship leader dreams of writing songs that shift atmospheres—his music eventually impacts millions.

Destiny dreams aren't just about personal success—they are about advancing God's kingdom.

How to Respond to a Destiny Dream

If you receive a dream that reveals something about your calling, here's how to steward it well:

1. Write the Dream Down

- Record every detail, including emotions and key symbols.
- Some destiny dreams take years to unfold, so keeping a record is important.

2. Seek Confirmation

- Does the dream align with what God has already been speaking to you?
- Does it match biblical patterns of how God calls people?
- Share it with mature believers or mentors who can provide insight.

3. Pray for Wisdom and Timing

- Not all dreams are meant to be acted on immediately.
- Ask God when and how to step into the calling revealed in the dream.

4. Prepare for Opposition and Growth

- Joseph had a destiny dream, but his path included trials, betrayal, and testing before fulfillment.
- Many destiny dreams require spiritual preparation, character development, and endurance.

5. Stay Faithful in Small Things

- Sometimes, God gives destiny dreams years before fulfillment.
- Be faithful where you are now—God will open doors at the right time.

Dreams Are a Glimpse of Your Calling

If God has given you a dream that reveals your future, treat it as a sacred invitation to walk in purpose. Destiny dreams are not about self-fulfillment—they are about aligning with God's plan for your life and His kingdom.

Are you paying attention to the dreams that reveal your calling?

Chapter 8

How to Properly Interpret a Dream
The Need for Interpretation

You WAKE UP FROM A VIVID DREAM, SENSING THAT IT WAS significant—but you don't know what it means. The images, symbols, and emotions felt real, but without understanding, they remain a mystery.

Dreams are one of God's ways of speaking, but they require interpretation. The Bible is filled with dreams that needed interpretation before their meaning was clear.

- Pharaoh had a dream of seven fat cows and seven thin cows—but only Joseph, through divine revelation, could interpret its meaning (Genesis 41 NKJV).
- Nebuchadnezzar dreamed of a great statue—but only Daniel could explain what it represented (Daniel 2 NKJV).
- Peter had a vision of unclean animals being lowered in a sheet—but it took a revelation from the

Holy Spirit to understand that it meant the inclusion of the Gentiles (Acts 10:9-16 NKJV).

Correct dream interpretation is not a guessing game—it is a process of spiritual discernment. In this chapter, we will walk through a biblical approach to interpreting dreams, ensuring that we understand what God is truly saying.

1. The Five Steps of Dream Interpretation

To properly interpret a dream, follow these five steps

Step 1: Write It Down – Keeping a Dream Journal

Dreams are often forgotten quickly, so it's crucial to write them down immediately.

- Record everything you remember, including:
- The setting (where were you?).
- The emotions (how did you feel?).
- The key symbols (objects, people, colors, numbers).
- Any conversations or words spoken in the dream.
- Keep a dedicated dream journal to track recurring symbols and patterns.

"And the Lord answered me: 'Write the vision; make it plain on tablets, so he may run who reads it.'" (Habakkuk 2:2)

Step 2: Identify the Key Elements

Not every detail in a dream is significant. Some aspects serve as background, while others carry spiritual meaning. Ask:

- What stood out the most in the dream?
- Were there any repeating elements?
- Did the dream feel symbolic or literal?

Example:

- If you dream of a door opening, the focus may be on transition or opportunity.
- If you dream of a lion, it could represent spiritual authority, Jesus, or an enemy depending on the context.

Step 3: Seek the Holy Spirit's Revelation

Dreams are spiritual messages and cannot be understood with natural reasoning alone. Ask the Holy Spirit for divine revelation:

"However, when He, the Spirit of truth, has come, He will guide you into all truth..." (John 16:13 NKJV)

How to seek revelation:

- Pray and ask, "Lord, what does this mean?"
- Meditate on Scripture—does the dream remind you of a biblical story or symbol?
- Wait for confirmation—sometimes the meaning unfolds over time.

Dreams should never contradict the Bible—God's voice in dreams will always align with His Word.

Step 4: Compare with Scripture

Many symbols in dreams have biblical foundations. Before assigning a meaning to something, check if the Bible provides a precedent.

- Water → Often represents the Holy Spirit, cleansing, or the Word of God (John 7:38, Ephesians 5:26).
- Fire → Can symbolize purification or God's presence (Malachi 3:2-3, Exodus 3:2).
- Sheep → Represent God's people (John 10:27).
- Snakes → Often symbolize deception or the enemy (Genesis 3:1).

When in doubt, align your interpretation with biblical truth.

<u>Step 5: Apply Wisdom and Discernment</u>

Not every dream is meant to be acted on immediately. Some require waiting, prayer, or deeper understanding. Ask:

- Is this dream personal (about my life) or corporate (about others, the church, or a nation)?
- Does this dream confirm something God has already been speaking?
- Should I take action, pray, or wait for further insight?

Example:

- If you dream of a car losing control, it could symbolize a season of transition or needing to trust

God's direction. Instead of acting impulsively, pray for clarity and seek wise counsel.

2. Personal vs. Corporate Dreams

Some dreams are meant for you personally, while others carry messages for a larger group (church, nation, leadership).

Personal Dreams

- Often relate to your spiritual journey, growth, or warnings.
- May include God's promises, corrections, or encouragements.

Example:

- Dreaming of climbing a mountain could mean God is calling you to a new spiritual challenge.

Corporate Dreams

- Often relate to a group of people, the church, or global events.
- Require confirmation and discernment before sharing.

Example:

- A dream of an earthquake hitting a city could be a call to intercede for that region.

If you believe your dream is corporate, seek wise counsel before sharing publicly.

"Surely the Lord God does nothing unless He reveals His secret to His servants the prophets." (*Amos 3:7 NKJV*)

3. Avoiding Common Mistakes in Dream Interpretation

Mistake #1: Assuming Every Dream is Literal
Not all dreams are meant to be taken at face value.

Example:

- Dreaming of a storm doesn't necessarily mean a physical storm is coming—it could symbolize spiritual warfare or personal turmoil.

Mistake #2: Ignoring the Emotional Tone
The feeling in a dream matters.

Example:

- Dreaming of fire with excitement and joy → Could mean God's presence and revival.
- Dreaming of fire with fear → Could symbolize destruction or judgment.

Mistake #3: Over-Relying on Dream Dictionaries
While biblical symbols are helpful, dreams are personal —God may use symbols uniquely based on your experiences.

Example:

- For some, a dog in a dream might mean loyalty.
- For others, it could symbolize a past trauma or fear.

Always seek God for the true meaning rather than relying solely on external sources.

4. What to Do After Interpreting a Dream

1. If the Dream Brings a Call to Action

- If it's a warning dream, pray and ask God how to respond.
- If it's directional, seek wise counsel before making decisions.

2. If the Dream Requires Waiting

- Some dreams are not meant to be acted upon immediately—they reveal future events or long-term callings.
- Keep a record of your dream and watch for confirmation.

3. If the Dream is a Call to Intercession

- Some dreams reveal spiritual warfare or intercessory assignments.
- If God shows you something about another person or a nation, pray before sharing.

Seeking Understanding from God

God is speaking through dreams, but correct interpretation requires wisdom, patience, and spiritual discernment. Rather than rushing to conclusions, we must pray, study Scripture, and listen to the Holy Spirit. The goal is not just to understand our dreams, but to grow in intimacy with the One who gives them.

Are you willing to go deeper in understanding the dreams God is speaking to you?

Chapter 9

Personal vs. Corporate Dreams
Understanding the Scope of Dreams

HAVE YOU EVER WOKEN UP FROM A DREAM AND wondered, Was that just for me, or is God speaking about something bigger?

Dreams can be deeply personal, revealing something about your spiritual life, your future, or your emotions. But sometimes, God gives dreams that reach beyond the individual, carrying messages for churches, nations, and even the global body of Christ. Knowing whether a dream is personal or corporate is crucial because it determines:

- How you respond—Do you pray privately, or do you share it with others?
- Who it's meant for—Is it just for your guidance, or is God speaking to a group?
- What action to take—Should you adjust your own life, or is it a call for intercession?

Many misinterpret dreams because they assume all dreams

are personal when in fact, some are meant to be shared. Others make the mistake of publicly declaring a dream that was meant for private prayer. This chapter will help you discern the difference between personal and corporate dreams and how to handle them with wisdom.

1. What Are Personal Dreams?

Definition: A personal dream is a dream in which God speaks specifically to an individual about their own life, walk with Him, or personal spiritual growth. These dreams:

- Are focused on you—your emotions, struggles, and relationship with God.
- Often reveal personal correction, direction, or encouragement.
- Usually contain symbols unique to your journey.
- Are not necessarily meant to be shared but are for your personal development.

<u>Biblical Examples of Personal Dreams</u>

1. Jacob's Ladder (Genesis 28:10-17). Jacob was on the run from his brother Esau when he had a dream of a ladder stretching from earth to heaven, with angels ascending and descending. In the dream, God reaffirmed His covenant with Jacob, promising to be with him.

- Personal revelation—It was about Jacob's destiny, not a prophecy for others.
- Encouragement and direction—God was reminding Jacob that his future was secure.

- Response: Jacob woke up and declared, "Surely the Lord is in this place, and I did not know it" (Genesis 28:16 NKJV).

This was not a dream for a nation or a people group—it was a personal encounter between Jacob and God.

2. Joseph's Dreams of Leadership (Genesis 37:5-11). Joseph had two dreams showing his future leadership, where his family members would bow before him.

- Personal destiny dream—God was revealing Joseph's calling.
- Mistake: Joseph shared his dream too soon, leading to jealousy and betrayal.

This teaches us that not all personal dreams should be shared immediately. Some are meant to be prayed over until the right time.

3. Solomon's Dream of Wisdom (1 Kings 3:5-15). King Solomon had a dream where God asked him what he wanted. He requested wisdom, and God granted it.

- A personal dream that altered his destiny.
- He acted upon the dream by ruling wisely.

This shows that personal dreams can bring transformation if responded to correctly.

How to Respond to a Personal Dream

1. Pray for interpretation – Ask God what the dream means for you.
2. Compare with Scripture – Does it align with biblical principles?
3. Seek confirmation – If unsure, ask a mature spiritual mentor.
4. Apply it to your life – Some dreams require action, others require patience.
5. Be careful with sharing – Not all dreams are meant for public discussion.

2. What Are Corporate Dreams?

Definition: A corporate dream is a dream in which God speaks about a church, organization, city, nation, or group of people. These dreams often contain messages of warning, encouragement, or direction for a larger audience. These dreams:

- Concern others—not just the dreamer.
- Require discernment before being shared.
- Often carry a burden for prayer, intercession, or repentance.

<u>Biblical Examples of Corporate Dreams</u>

1. Pharaoh's Dream of Famine (Genesis 41:1-32). Pharaoh dreamed of seven fat cows and seven thin cows, and later, seven healthy stalks of grain and seven withered ones.

- This was not about Pharaoh personally—it was a warning for an entire nation.

- Joseph interpreted the dream and prepared Egypt for the coming famine.
- Without action, the dream would have been meaningless.

2. Nebuchadnezzar's Dream of the Statue (Daniel 2:31-45). Nebuchadnezzar dreamed of a giant statue made of different metals, which symbolized future world empires.

- A prophetic dream concerning the world's future.
- Daniel's interpretation brought clarity and divine insight.

This shows that corporate dreams often reveal large-scale events beyond the dreamer's personal life.

3. Pilate's Wife's Dream (Matthew 27:19). Pilate's wife had a dream warning her husband not to condemn Jesus.

- This was not a personal dream—it had consequences for the entire world.
- Pilate ignored it, showing that corporate warnings should not be dismissed.

3. How to Handle a Corporate Dream

Step 1: Pray for Discernment

Not every corporate dream is meant to be immediately shared. Ask:

- Is this dream truly from God?
- Does this require prayer, intercession, or action?

Step 2: Seek Wise Counsel

Corporate dreams should be processed in community. Share with:

- A mentor, pastor, or prophetic leader.
- Other mature believers who can help discern the message.

"Let two or three prophets speak, and let the others judge." (1 Corinthians 14:29)

Step 3: If Released to Share, Do So with Wisdom

When God confirms you should share a corporate dream:

- Do not cause unnecessary fear.
- Present it humbly and biblically.
- Encourage prayer and response rather than panic.

Example:

- If you dream of a coming disaster, the correct response may be intercession rather than public alarm.
- If you dream of revival, it may be a call for preparation and unity.

4. What Happens If Corporate Dreams Are Ignored?

Throughout history, God has warned nations through dreams, and those warnings were either heeded or ignored.

When Dreams Were Obeyed:

- Joseph interpreted Pharaoh's dream, saving Egypt from famine.
- Daniel interpreted Nebuchadnezzar's dream, bringing wisdom to Babylon.

When Dreams Were Ignored:

- Nebuchadnezzar ignored a dream warning him of pride—he lost his kingdom for seven years.
- Pilate ignored his wife's warning—he condemned Jesus.

Ignoring corporate dreams can have serious consequences, while responding in wisdom aligns us with God's will.

Discerning Between Personal and Corporate Dreams

Key Takeaways:

- Personal dreams focus on your walk with God, calling, or spiritual growth.
- Corporate dreams concern churches, leaders, or nations.
- Not all dreams should be shared immediately— some require prayer and confirmation.
- Corporate dreams often require intercession before public declaration.

God is still speaking through dreams—are you handling them with wisdom?

Chapter 10

Seeking Counsel in Dream Interpretation

The Importance of Seeking Wise Counsel

DREAMS ARE A DIVINE MYSTERY—HEAVENLY MESSAGES often wrapped in symbols, metaphors, and parables. While God sometimes gives clear and direct revelation, most dreams require interpretation. Even the greatest biblical dreamers—Joseph, Daniel, and Peter—did not always understand their dreams immediately. This is why seeking wise counsel is crucial. Dreams are not meant to be interpreted in isolation. Proverbs 11:14 (NKJV) states:

"Where there is no counsel, the people fall; but in the multitude of counselors there is safety."

Seeking godly, mature counsel helps ensure that we:

- Avoid misinterpretation.
- Receive confirmation.
- Stay accountable in our discernment.
- Do not act prematurely on an unclear dream.

Many believers either ignore their dreams or assume their own understanding is correct without seeking wise interpretation. Both extremes can lead to missed opportunities or missteps in spiritual decision-making. This chapter will explore:

1. Why we need wise counsel in dream interpretation.
2. Biblical examples of seeking interpretation from others.
3. How to discern who should interpret our dreams.
4. How to test and confirm a dream's meaning.

Why We Need Counsel in Dream Interpretation
Dreams Are Often Symbolic, Not Literal

Dreams are rarely direct messages—they require spiritual discernment. Many times, symbols, actions, and settings need interpretation before we understand their meaning.

Biblical Example:

- Joseph's dream of ruling over his brothers (Genesis 37:5-11) was not about literal bowing but about his future position of leadership in Egypt.
- Nebuchadnezzar's dream of a statue (Daniel 2) wasn't about an actual idol but represented successive world empires.

If we take dreams literally without interpretation, we may misapply their meaning. Seeking wise counsel ensures we interpret correctly.

Misinterpretation Can Lead to Mistakes

Without wise counsel, we risk misapplying a dream's message.

Biblical Example:

- Peter's vision of unclean animals (Acts 10:9-16)
- At first, Peter thought the dream was about food laws.
- But through wise revelation, he realized it symbolized God's acceptance of Gentiles into the Church.

A wrong interpretation could have led to Peter missing a major shift in God's kingdom. This proves that without proper guidance, we might misunderstand what God is saying.

Biblical Examples of Seeking Dream Interpretation

1. Joseph Interprets Pharaoh's Dream (Genesis 41:1-32). Pharaoh had two troubling dreams of seven fat cows followed by seven thin cows and seven healthy stalks of grain followed by withered stalks.

- Pharaoh could not interpret the dream.
- His magicians and advisors failed to explain it.
- Joseph, with God's wisdom, correctly interpreted it, revealing that the dream foretold seven years of abundance followed by seven years of famine.

This shows that not everyone has the gift of interpretation—even rulers and scholars needed a spiritually gifted interpreter.

Lesson: If a corporate leader like Pharaoh needed help interpreting his dreams, so do we!

2. Daniel Interprets Nebuchadnezzar's Dream (Daniel 2:1-45). King Nebuchadnezzar had a disturbing dream but forgot its details. He demanded his advisors tell him the dream and interpret it, or he would have them executed.

- His magicians and wise men failed.
- Daniel sought God, received revelation, and interpreted the dream correctly.
- His interpretation revealed the rise and fall of future world empires.

This example shows that:

- Some dreams require revelation beyond human understanding.
- God uses spiritually gifted people to interpret complex dreams.
- Seeking wisdom from the right source is essential.

How to Discern Who Should Interpret Your Dreams

Not everyone is qualified to interpret dreams. Here's how to choose the right person:

<u>Seek Someone Spiritually Mature</u>

Not all believers have the spiritual depth to interpret dreams correctly. Look for someone who:

- Is spiritually grounded in the Word.
- Has a track record of accuracy in discernment.
- Is led by the Holy Spirit, not personal opinions.

Biblical Example:

- Daniel was chosen over Babylon's magicians because of his godly wisdom.
- Joseph was recognized for his ability to interpret dreams with divine revelation.

A spiritually mature interpreter will point you to God's will, not their own biases.

Avoid False Interpreters or Self-Appointed "Experts"

Be cautious of people who:

- Claim every dream means something prophetic.
- Rely on dream dictionaries alone without seeking God.
- Interpret dreams based on personal opinions rather than biblical principles.

Example:
King Saul sought a medium instead of God, leading to disastrous consequences (1 Samuel 28:7-20). If you seek interpretation from the wrong source, you may receive distorted or misleading guidance.

Seek Confirmation from Multiple Sources

Even when you receive an interpretation, seek confirmation from:

- Prayer and Scripture—Does the meaning align with God's Word?
- Other mature believers—Do they confirm the interpretation?
- The Holy Spirit—Do you have peace about it?

Biblical Principle:

"By the mouth of two or three witnesses, every word shall be established." (*2 Corinthians 13:1 NKJV*)

If an interpretation feels off, forced, or leads to confusion, it may not be from God.

Testing and Confirming a Dream's Meaning

Not all dreams require immediate action. Before acting on a dream, test it using these biblical principles:

Does It Align with Scripture?

If a dream leads you toward righteousness, repentance, or wisdom, it is likely from God. If it contradicts God's Word, moral principles, or sound doctrine, it is NOT from Him.

Example:

- A dream encouraging bitterness or revenge is NOT from God.

- A dream calling you to repentance and holiness aligns with God's nature.

Does It Bear Spiritual Fruit?

Jesus said: *"You will know them by their fruits."* (*Matthew 7:16 NKJV*)

Ask yourself:

- Does the interpretation bring peace and clarity or confusion and fear?
- Does it lead to Christ-centered growth?

Does It Confirm What God Is Already Saying?

Most dreams confirm what God has already spoken through:

- Scripture
- Prayer
- Prophetic words or personal revelation

If a dream contradicts everything God has previously shown you, test it carefully.

Does It Require Action or Just Prayer?

Some dreams call for:

- Immediate action (e.g., warning dreams).
- Long-term preparation (e.g., Joseph's destiny dreams).

- Prayer and intercession only (e.g., corporate warning dreams).

Avoid acting rashly on unclear dreams—wait for confirmation!

Seeking Counsel Leads to Greater Understanding

Dreams are powerful messages from God, but without proper interpretation, they can be misunderstood or misused. Seeking wise, godly counsel in dream interpretation:

- Helps avoid misinterpretation.
- Brings confirmation and clarity.
- Keeps us accountable in decision-making.
- Aligns us with God's will and timing.

Instead of rushing to conclusions, seek wisdom, confirmation, and the Holy Spirit's leading. God doesn't just want to give you dreams—He wants to give you understanding.

Are you seeking wise counsel in your dream life?

Chapter 11

Responding to Dreams in Prayer and Action

The Right Response to a God-Given Dream

DREAMS ARE NOT JUST FOR INFORMATION—THEY REQUIRE a response. Whether a dream is a warning, a call to action, or an invitation to deeper intimacy with God, how we respond determines whether we fully benefit from what God is revealing.

Many believers receive profound dreams but fail to act on them. Some forget their dreams, while others dismiss them as random thoughts. Others may misunderstand the dream's meaning and either act prematurely or ignore an important revelation.

Throughout the Bible, God gave dreams with specific purposes, and in nearly every case, the dreamer had to respond with obedience, prayer, or preparation. In this chapter, we will explore:

1. How to discern whether a dream requires action or prayer.

2. Biblical examples of right and wrong responses to dreams.
3. Practical steps to responding correctly.
4. How to engage in prophetic intercession based on dreams.

When we take our dreams seriously and respond with wisdom, we open the door for God's guidance, protection, and blessings.

How to Discern Whether a Dream Requires Action or Prayer

Not every dream requires an immediate action. Some dreams are meant to:

- Warn and prepare us (e.g., Joseph being warned to flee with baby Jesus).
- Direct and guide us (e.g., Paul's Macedonian call).
- Call us to intercession (e.g., Abraham interceding for Sodom).
- Reveal something for future seasons (e.g., Joseph's dreams of ruling Egypt).

Before responding to a dream, ask these five key questions:

1. Is the Dream a Call to Immediate Action?

Some dreams demand urgent action because they contain warnings or divine instructions.

Example: Joseph Warned to Flee (Matthew 2:13-14)

- Joseph was warned in a dream to take Mary and Jesus to Egypt because Herod was seeking to kill the child.
- He immediately obeyed, fleeing to Egypt at night.

When a dream contains a clear warning or instruction, obey immediately.

2. Is the Dream Calling You to Change or Repent?

Some dreams reveal areas where we need repentance or spiritual growth.

Example: Nebuchadnezzar's Warning Dream (Daniel 4:4-37)

- He dreamed of a great tree being cut down, symbolizing his own prideful fall.
- He ignored the warning and later suffered judgment.

When a dream calls you to repentance, respond with humility before God.

3. Is the Dream for Future Preparation?

Some dreams reveal events or assignments that will unfold in the future.

Example: Pharaoh's Dream of Famine (Genesis 41:1-32)

- The dream foretold seven years of plenty followed by seven years of famine.
- Joseph responded by preparing Egypt for the famine.

When a dream reveals future events, seek God for how to prepare.

4. Is the Dream a Call to Intercession?

Some dreams show us things that need to be prayed over rather than acted upon.

Example: Abraham Interceding for Sodom (Genesis 18:16-33 NKJV)

- Though not a dream, Abraham received a divine revelation about Sodom's destruction.
- Instead of rushing to warn Sodom, he interceded for mercy.

When a dream shows danger or judgment, seek God in intercessory prayer.

5. Is the Dream a Confirmation?

Some dreams confirm what God has already been speaking through Scripture, prophecy, or life circumstances.

Example: Paul's Macedonian Call (Acts 16:9-10)

- Paul had a vision of a man from Macedonia calling for help.

- This dream confirmed his next missionary journey.

If a dream confirms what God has already been showing you, move forward with faith.

Biblical Examples of Right and Wrong Responses to Dreams

Right Responses to Dreams

Joseph's Dream of Leadership (Genesis 37:5-11 NKJV)

- Joseph believed in his dream but had to endure trials before its fulfillment.
- He remained faithful, and God's promise came to pass.

Daniel's Interpretation of Dreams (Daniel 2 & 4)

- Daniel sought God's wisdom before interpreting the king's dream.
- His humility and accuracy saved lives and advanced God's kingdom.

Peter's Vision of the Unclean Animals (Acts 10:9-16)

- Peter was confused at first but waited for confirmation.
- He obeyed God's leading, opening the gospel to the Gentiles.

<u>Wrong Responses to Dreams</u>

Nebuchadnezzar's Prideful Response (Daniel 4)

- He was warned in a dream but refused to humble himself.
- He was driven into the wilderness until he repented.

Pilate Ignoring His Wife's Dream (Matthew 27:19)

- Pilate's wife was warned in a dream about Jesus.
- Pilate ignored the warning and condemned Christ.

Pharaoh's Magicians Misinterpreting Dreams (Exodus 7:11-12)

- Pharaoh's magicians and sorcerers tried to interpret divine signs but failed.
- Not everyone is qualified to interpret dreams—seek godly counsel.

Practical Steps for Responding to Dreams

Step 1: Write It Down Immediately

- Record every detail, emotion, and key symbol.
- Keep a dream journal to recognize patterns over time.

Step 2: Seek Interpretation Through Prayer

- Ask, "Holy Spirit, what does this dream mean?"

- Compare with biblical dream patterns (Joseph, Daniel, Peter).
- If unclear, wait on God for confirmation.

Step 3: Compare with Scripture

- Dreams from God never contradict His Word.
- Use biblical symbolism to discern the message.

Step 4: Seek Wise Counsel

- Share with trusted spiritual mentors, pastors, or prophetic leaders.
- Avoid self-appointed interpreters or those without biblical grounding.

Step 5: Determine the Right Response

- Obey immediately if the dream calls for action.
- Repent if the dream reveals a spiritual issue.
- Prepare if the dream speaks of future events.
- Intercede if the dream is a warning for others.

Engaging in Prophetic Intercession for Dreams

Many dreams are given not for immediate action, but for intercession.

How to Intercede Based on a Dream:

- Pray in the Spirit—Ask the Holy Spirit to reveal how to pray.

- Declare God's will—Speak God's promises over the situation.
- Fast if needed—Some dreams require deeper spiritual warfare.
- Partner with others—Join intercessory groups to pray over corporate dreams.

Example:

- If you dream of a natural disaster, pray for mercy and protection over that region.
- If you dream of a leader making a wrong decision, intercede for wisdom and guidance.

Intercession shifts outcomes—many warnings in Scripture were reversed through prayer!

Faithful Stewardship of Dreams

Dreams are not just messages to observe—they require response. Whether through obedience, intercession, preparation, or repentance, how we handle our dreams determines whether we align with God's purposes.

- Write them down.
- Pray for wisdom and discernment.
- Compare them with Scripture.
- Seek wise counsel.
- Act in obedience.

When we respond rightly to dreams, we partner with God's voice and plans for our lives and the world. How are you responding to the dreams God is speaking to you?

Chapter 12

Dream Journaling and Record-Keeping

Why Documenting Your Dreams is Essential

DREAMS ARE DIVINE MESSAGES, BUT IF WE DON'T RECORD them, we risk forgetting or misinterpreting what God is saying. Many believers receive life-changing dreams but fail to capture the details, leading to missed revelation and lost direction. The Bible emphasizes the importance of writing down divine revelations:

> *"Then the Lord answered me and said: 'Write the vision and make it plain on tablets, that he may run who reads it.'"*
> (*Habakkuk 2:2 NKJV*)

God expects us to steward revelation well, including dreams. Keeping a dream journal is a practical way to:

- Recognize recurring patterns and symbols.
- Track the fulfillment of prophetic dreams.
- Receive deeper understanding over time.
- Avoid forgetting significant details.

In this chapter, we will explore:

1. Why keeping a dream journal is important.
2. How to properly record and organize dreams.
3. How to identify recurring themes and prophetic patterns.
4. How dream journaling strengthens spiritual discernment.

If you are serious about growing in dream interpretation, a dream journal is one of your most valuable tools.

Why Keep a Dream Journal?

<u>Dreams Are Easily Forgotten</u>

Science shows that 90% of dreams are forgotten within 10 minutes of waking. If we do not immediately document our dreams, details will fade, and we may lose vital revelation.

Example: Daniel's Dreams and Visions (Daniel 7:1 NKJV)

"In the first year of Belshazzar king of Babylon, Daniel had a dream and visions of his head while on his bed. Then he wrote down the dream, telling the main facts."

Daniel did not rely on memory—he wrote down his dreams, ensuring they were preserved for interpretation and fulfillment.

<u>Dreams Contain Layers of Meaning</u>

Many dreams are not understood fully at first. Over time, as events unfold and God provides more clarity, recorded dreams can take on new significance.

Example: Joseph's Destiny Dreams (Genesis 37:5-11)

- Joseph's dreams about his brothers bowing to him made no sense at first.
- Years later, when he became a ruler in Egypt, they were fulfilled.

If he had dismissed or forgotten them, he might have failed to recognize God's plan. Recording your dreams allows for deeper understanding as they unfold.

God Speaks Through Patterns Over Time

God often reveals messages through multiple dreams over weeks, months, or years. Without a journal, it's difficult to see patterns and repeated themes.

Example: Pharaoh's Two Dreams (Genesis 41:25-32 NKJV)

- Pharaoh had two dreams about famine, confirming that the event was certain to happen.
- Joseph saw the pattern and knew it was time to prepare.

Keeping a journal helps you recognize when God is emphasizing a message through repetition.

How to Properly Record and Organize Dreams

A dream journal is more than just writing down dreams—it involves a structured approach to documentation and reflection.

<u>What to Include in Your Dream Journal</u>
Each dream entry should contain:

- Date & Time – When did the dream occur? (This helps track timing and fulfillment.)
- Dream Title – A short phrase summarizing the dream's main theme.
- Emotional Tone – How did you feel during and after the dream?
- Dream Description – Write every detail you can remember.
- Symbols & Key Elements – List important objects, people, colors, or numbers.
- Possible Interpretation – Write any initial thoughts on what the dream might mean.
- Scriptures or Prophetic Connections – Does the dream connect with a Bible passage or previous revelation?
- Follow-Up Actions – Does the dream require prayer, intercession, or action?

<u>Example Dream Journal Entry</u>

Date: March 15, 2025
Title: The Open Door and the Golden Key
Emotions: Peaceful, expectant

Dream Description:
I was standing in front of a large golden door. I saw a
bright golden key in my hand. As I placed the key into
the lock, the door opened, and a wave of light came
through. I stepped inside, and I heard a voice say, "A
new season has begun."

Symbols & Key Elements:

- Golden key → Symbol of access, authority, and
  unlocking new opportunities.
- Open door → Transition into a new season.
- Wave of light → Divine revelation, the presence
  of God.

Possible Interpretation:
I believe this dream represents a coming breakthrough in
my spiritual journey. The key could symbolize wisdom or a
new opportunity that God is giving me.

Scriptural Connection:

"I have set before you an open door, which no one can shut."
(Revelation 3:8 NKJV)

Follow-Up Actions:

- Pray for clarity on what "new season" God is
  leading me into.
- Stay sensitive to divine opportunities in the coming
  weeks.

Tools for Effective Dream Journaling

You can use:

- A physical notebook (great for handwriting notes).
- A digital journal (apps like Evernote, OneNote, or Notion).
- Voice recordings (recording your dreams upon waking if you don't have time to write).

Whatever method you choose, be consistent in recording every significant dream.

How to Identify Recurring Themes and Patterns in Dreams

When you consistently document dreams, patterns begin to emerge.

Recognizing Repeated Symbols
If you keep dreaming about:

- A storm → It could represent a coming trial.
- A wedding → It could symbolize union with Christ or preparation.
- A staircase → It could represent spiritual promotion or transition.

Repeated symbols indicate something God is highlighting.

Identifying Repeated Messages

Sometimes, God repeats a dream with variations. This is a sign that the message is urgent.

Example: Pharaoh's Dreams (Genesis 41:32 NKJV)

"And the dream was repeated to Pharaoh twice because the thing is established by God, and God will shortly bring it to pass."

If you have multiple dreams with similar themes, take them seriously!

<u>Noticing Timing and Fulfillment</u>

Keeping a journal helps you track:

- How long it takes for a dream to be fulfilled.
- Whether a past dream is coming true in your life.

Example:

- You dream of leading a ministry, but it makes no sense now.
- Years later, you find yourself stepping into that very role.

If you didn't record the dream, you might miss recognizing its fulfillment.

How Dream Journaling Strengthens Spiritual Discernment

<u>Discern the Source of Dreams</u>

By tracking your dreams, you begin to recognize:

- Which dreams are from God.
- Which dreams are from your soul (personal thoughts/emotions).
- Which dreams are from the enemy (deceptive, fear-inducing dreams).

Over time, you become more accurate in dream interpretation.

<u>Recognizing God's Voice More Clearly</u>

The more you record and study dreams, the more you understand how God speaks to you personally.

"My sheep hear My voice, and I know them, and they follow Me." (John 10:27 NKJV)

Dream journaling helps you develop sensitivity to God's voice in all areas of life.

Stewarding the Prophetic Language of Dreams

Dreams are divine invitations—they require stewardship, prayer, and wisdom. Keeping a dream journal is not just a habit; it is a way of valuing and responding to God's voice. Key Takeaways:

- Write down every significant dream.
- Look for recurring patterns and themes.
- Pray for wisdom in interpretation.
- Recognize fulfillment over time.

When you steward your dreams well, you position yourself to hear from God more clearly and walk in greater revelation. Are you keeping a record of what God is speaking to you in the night?

Chapter 13

Dreams as a Tool for Spiritual Warfare

How Dreams Reveal the Battle in the Spiritual Realm

DREAMS ARE NOT JUST MESSAGES OF ENCOURAGEMENT OR guidance—they are often spiritual battlegrounds where God reveals hidden conflicts, demonic attacks, and divine strategies for victory. Many believers do not realize that their dreams can be a weapon of warfare in their fight against the enemy. Throughout Scripture, God gave dreams to:

- Expose the enemy's plans before they unfolded.
- Prepare His people for spiritual battles.
- Empower believers to stand against demonic attacks.
- Equip intercessors with insight for strategic prayer.

If we dismiss our dreams as random thoughts, we may miss crucial warnings and divine instructions for warfare. When we learn to recognize spiritual attacks in dreams and respond with authority, we become more effective in the battle against darkness. In this chapter, we will explore:

1. How the enemy tries to attack through dreams.
2. How God reveals demonic strategies through dreams.
3. Biblical examples of dreams as tools for warfare.
4. How to fight back using prayer, fasting, and spiritual authority.

God wants you to be victorious in spiritual warfare, and dreams are one of the ways He equips you for battle.

How the Enemy Attacks Through Dreams

Satan knows that dreams are a powerful way God communicates, so he tries to infiltrate our dreams with lies, fear, and deception.

<u>Types of Demonic Dreams</u>

Nightmares and Fear-Inducing Dreams

- The enemy often sends dreams filled with terror, panic, or death to instill fear.
- These dreams can cause anxiety, sleeplessness, or a spirit of oppression.

Example: Job's Tormenting Dreams (Job 7:14 NKJV)

"Then You scare me with dreams and terrify me with visions."

Solution: Pray before sleeping, rebuke fear, and stand in the authority of Christ.

<u>Sexual or Lustful Dreams</u>

- The enemy sometimes introduces impure or sexual dreams to defile a believer's spirit.
- These dreams may attempt to bring temptation, soul ties, or demonic oppression.

Solution: If you wake up from such a dream, immediately repent, renounce any ungodly influence, and break any potential demonic attachment.

Dreams That Bring Confusion or False Direction

- Satan can disguise himself as "an angel of light" to deceive (2 Corinthians 11:14 NKJV).
- Some dreams appear prophetic but lead to deception if not tested against Scripture.

Solution: Always compare dreams with the Bible. If a dream contradicts God's Word, it is not from Him.

Dreams That Bring Oppression or Sleep Paralysis

- Some people experience dark, paralyzing dreams where they feel unable to move, speak, or wake up.
- This is often a demonic attack meant to instill fear and create spiritual bondage.

Solution: Call on the name of Jesus, plead the blood of Christ over your sleep, and pray for deliverance.

How God Reveals Demonic Strategies Through Dreams

While Satan tries to attack in dreams, God also uses dreams to expose the enemy's plans before they unfold.

Example: The Enemy's Attack on Israel Revealed in a Dream (Judges 7:13-15)

- A Midianite soldier dreamed of a barley loaf rolling into their camp and destroying them.
- Gideon overheard the dream and realized God had already given him victory.
- Because of this prophetic dream, Gideon went into battle with confidence and defeated the Midianites.

Lesson: God can reveal the enemy's defeat before the battle even begins!

Biblical Examples of Dreams as Spiritual Warfare

Joseph's Dream to Flee from Herod (Matthew 2:13-15)

- God warned Joseph in a dream that Herod wanted to kill baby Jesus.
- Joseph obeyed and took Jesus to Egypt, escaping the enemy's trap.

Lesson: Dreams can serve as divine protection against the enemy's schemes.

Pilate's Wife's Dream About Jesus (Matthew 27:19)

- Pilate's wife had a dream warning her husband not to condemn Jesus.

- Pilate ignored the warning, and Jesus was crucified.

Lesson: Ignoring warning dreams can lead to spiritual consequences.

<u>Daniel's Night Visions (Daniel 7:1-28)</u>

- Daniel had prophetic dreams that revealed the rise and fall of world empires.
- These dreams exposed the spiritual battle behind earthly governments.

Lesson: God reveals the unseen spiritual realm through dreams.

How to Fight Back Against Demonic Attacks in Dreams

If you experience demonic dreams, nightmares, or spiritual attacks while sleeping, there are powerful ways to fight back using the weapons of spiritual warfare.

<u>Cover Your Sleep in Prayer</u>

Before sleeping, pray:

"Lord, I cover my mind, body, and spirit in the blood of Jesus. I declare that my sleep belongs to You, and no demonic interference can enter my dreams. I reject every scheme of the enemy and receive divine revelation instead. In Jesus' name, amen."

This prayer shuts the door to demonic attacks in your sleep.

Declare Spiritual Authority Over Your Dreams

Jesus has given us authority over all the power of the enemy (Luke 10:19). If you have a disturbing dream, wake up and say:

"I rebuke every lie, fear, or attack from the enemy. I cancel any demonic influence in my dreams. I stand in the authority of Christ and declare my sleep belongs to the Lord. Satan, you have no access to my mind or spirit. I break every stronghold in Jesus' name!"

Speaking with authority breaks the power of demonic dreams.

Use Scripture as a Weapon

When Jesus was tempted by Satan, He responded with the Word of God (Matthew 4:1-11). Scripture is a powerful weapon against spiritual attacks in dreams. Key verses to declare before sleeping:

- Psalm 91:5-6 – "You shall not be afraid of the terror by night..."
- 2 Timothy 1:7 – "For God has not given us a spirit of fear..."
- Isaiah 54:17 – "No weapon formed against you shall prosper..."

Declaring Scripture before bed fortifies your spirit against enemy attacks.

Fasting and Prayer for Deliverance

If demonic dreams persist, consider fasting and seeking deliverance.

Example: Daniel Fasted for Revelation (Daniel 10:2-3, 12-14)

- Daniel fasted and prayed for understanding of a dream.
- The angel told him his prayer had been resisted by demonic forces.
- Fasting broke the resistance, and Daniel received divine revelation.

Lesson: If you are experiencing intense warfare in dreams, fasting strengthens your spiritual breakthrough.

Anoint Your Bedroom and Declare It as Holy Ground

- Pray over your bedroom and bed, dedicating them to the Lord.
- Anoint your room with oil as a symbol of God's protection.
- Declare, "My home is a dwelling place of God's presence. No evil spirit can enter here."

This establishes spiritual protection over your sleeping space.

Using Dreams as a Weapon in Spiritual Warfare

Dreams are not just random experiences—they are tools for spiritual warfare. Through dreams, God can:

- Expose the enemy's plans.
- Give warnings and strategies for victory.
- Empower us to take authority over demonic attacks.

Key Takeaways:

- Recognize when dreams are from the enemy and fight back with prayer.
- Use the name of Jesus and Scripture as weapons against demonic dreams.
- Steward prophetic warfare dreams by interceding and acting on divine warnings.

When we learn to engage in spiritual warfare through our dreams, we walk in greater authority, discernment, and victory. Are you using your dreams as a weapon in the battle against darkness?

Chapter 14

Cultivating a Lifestyle of Prophetic Dreams

How to Invite God to Speak Through Dreams Regularly

GOD IS ALWAYS SPEAK ING, BUT MANY BELIEVERS FAIL TO recognize His voice in dreams because they have not cultivated an awareness or expectation of Him speaking in the night. Prophetic dreams are not just occasional experiences—they can be a lifestyle. Throughout Scripture, those who consistently heard from God in dreams were those who:

- Walked closely with Him (Joseph, Daniel, Solomon).
- Sought understanding through prayer and interpretation (Daniel 2:18-19).
- Valued and recorded their dreams (Habakkuk 2:2).

If we position ourselves to receive, God will increase our capacity to hear Him in dreams. This chapter will explore:

1. How to position yourself to receive more prophetic dreams.

2. Practical habits to cultivate a dream-filled life.
3. The connection between purity, prayer, and prophetic dreams.
4. How to discern and increase the frequency of God-given dreams.

If you desire greater clarity and consistency in hearing God through dreams, there are biblical principles you can apply to cultivate a lifestyle of prophetic dreams.

Positioning Yourself to Receive More Prophetic Dreams

God Desires to Speak in the Night

God is always speaking, but many believers are spiritually "asleep" to His voice. He desires to reveal wisdom, warning, and direction through dreams.

Example: God's Promise of Dreams in the Last Days (Joel 2:28 NKJV)

"And it shall come to pass afterward that I will pour out My Spirit on all flesh; your sons and your daughters shall prophesy, your old men shall dream dreams, your young men shall see visions."

This verse confirms that dreams are an active part of the prophetic outpouring of the Holy Spirit. Those who are aligned with God's Spirit will receive divine dreams.

Ask God for Prophetic Dreams

Many believers never experience prophetic dreams simply because they never ask. If you desire to hear from God in dreams, pray and invite Him to speak.

Example: Solomon Asked for Wisdom, and God Spoke in a Dream (1 Kings 3:5-15)

- Solomon did not receive a random dream—he had positioned his heart to seek divine wisdom.
- Because he valued revelation, God responded through a dream.

Before sleeping, pray: "Lord, I invite You to speak to me in dreams. I am listening."

Expect to Hear From God

Faith and expectation attract revelation. When we expect to hear from God in dreams, we create an open channel for Him to speak.

Example: Daniel Actively Sought Understanding (Daniel 2:19-22)

- When Nebuchadnezzar had a dream, Daniel expected God to give him the interpretation.
- His expectation led to divine revelation.

Go to sleep believing God will speak. Keep a journal by your bedside, ready to write down anything He reveals.

Practical Habits to Cultivate a Dream-Filled Life

If you want to receive and understand more prophetic dreams, you must build habits that cultivate a spirit of revelation.

Maintain a Consistent Prayer Life

Prayer opens the heavens over your life. Those who regularly hear from God in dreams are those who spend time in His presence. Practical Step: Dedicate time before bed to prayer, asking God to give you divine insight through dreams.

Keep a Dream Journal and Record Every Dream

Many people miss important revelation simply because they fail to document their dreams. Practical Step:

- Keep a notebook or a digital journal by your bed.
- Write down every significant dream.
- Review past dreams to identify patterns and recurring themes.

"Write the vision and make it plain on tablets, that he may run who reads it." (Habakkuk 2:2 NKJV)

Recording your dreams shows God that you value what He is saying.

Eliminate Distractions Before Bed

The enemy will try to clutter your mind before sleep so you are less receptive to divine dreams. Avoid these distractions before bed:

- Excessive TV, social media, or news that fills your mind with unnecessary noise.
- Unresolved stress, anger, or sin, which can cloud your spiritual sensitivity.
- Fear-based or demonic movies, music, or conversations, which can attract dark influences into your dream life.

Practical Step:

- Spend 10-15 minutes before bed in worship, prayer, or reading Scripture.
- Speak peace over your mind, rejecting any distractions.

"You will keep him in perfect peace, whose mind is stayed on You, because he trusts in You." (Isaiah 26:3 NKJV)

The Connection Between Purity, Prayer, and Prophetic Dreams

Many believers block their dream life because they have unresolved sin, distractions, or impurity clouding their spirit.

Purity Increases Revelation

Jesus said: *"Blessed are the pure in heart, for they shall see God."* (Matthew 5:8)

If we want to see God in our dreams, we must maintain a pure heart and mind. Practical Step:

- If you struggle with lust, anger, or fear-based dreams, examine if there are areas where you need repentance and cleansing.
- Ask God to purify your heart so you can receive clearer, uncontaminated revelation.

<u>Fasting and Prayer Increase Spiritual Sensitivity</u>

When Daniel sought a higher level of prophetic revelation, he fasted for 21 days (Daniel 10:2-3). Practical Step:

- If you feel spiritually blocked, consider fasting to heighten your sensitivity to divine dreams.
- Ask God to remove any hindrances that block revelation.

How to Discern and Increase the Frequency of Prophetic Dreams

<u>Recognizing God's Voice in Dreams</u>

As you cultivate a lifestyle of prophetic dreams, you will begin to recognize:

- When a dream is from God.
- When a dream is just from your soul or subconscious.
- When the enemy is trying to infiltrate your dreams.

Practical Step:

- Always test your dreams against Scripture.

- Ask, "Does this dream align with God's character and His Word?"

How to Increase the Frequency of Prophetic Dreams

If you want to receive more frequent prophetic dreams, consistently apply these practices:

- Pray before bed, inviting God to speak.
- Write down every significant dream, no matter how small.
- Seek interpretation through prayer, Scripture, and wise counsel.
- Keep a lifestyle of purity and spiritual discipline.
- Eliminate distractions that hinder dream clarity.
- Thank God for every revelation you receive.

Living a Life of Prophetic Dreams

Dreams are not just occasional events—they can be a daily means of communication with God. If we steward our dream life well, God will entrust us with even greater revelation. Key Takeaways:

- Expect God to speak in dreams.
- Prepare your heart through prayer and purity.
- Keep a record of your dreams and seek interpretation.
- Remove distractions that hinder revelation.
- Take action on the dreams God gives you.

When you cultivate a lifestyle of prophetic dreams, you

become more aligned with God's voice, purposes, and kingdom assignments. Are you positioning yourself to receive from God in the night?

Conclusion: Awakening to the Voice of God in the Night

Embracing the Supernatural Language of Dreams

From the very beginning of creation, God has spoken through dreams. Throughout Scripture, He used the night season to reveal His will, warn His people, and guide them into their destinies. Today, He is still speaking—but are we listening?

Many believers treat dreams as random thoughts of the subconscious, unaware that God has designed dreams as a divine communication channel. Others recognize that God speaks through dreams but fail to steward them properly, leaving prophetic revelations unrecorded or un-acted upon.

Now that we have explored the biblical foundation, purpose, and interpretation of dreams, the question remains: How will you respond to God's voice in the night? This conclusion will help solidify:

1. Why dreams are essential for spiritual growth.

2. How to continue growing in dream interpretation.
3. The responsibility of stewarding divine revelation.
4. A final call to awaken to the supernatural realm of dreams.

God is always speaking—and when you embrace the prophetic language of the night, you will walk in deeper intimacy, revelation, and divine purpose.

Why Dreams Are Essential for Spiritual Growth

<u>Dreams Deepen Our Relationship With God</u>

Dreams are not just about prophecy, warnings, or direction —they are about relationship. When God speaks in a dream, He is inviting you into deeper communion with Him.

Example: Solomon's Dream of Wisdom (1 Kings 3:5-15)

- God appeared to Solomon in a dream, asking him what he desired.
- Solomon's request for wisdom pleased God, and he was blessed with unmatched understanding.
- This dream marked the beginning of Solomon's extraordinary leadership.

Lesson: God wants to speak to you in dreams, but He also wants a deeper relationship with you.

<u>Dreams Reveal Hidden Things and Callings</u>

Many people struggle with direction, calling, and purpose.

Dreams can serve as divine roadmaps, giving clarity about one's destiny.

Example: Joseph's Destiny Dreams (Genesis 37:5-11)

- As a young man, Joseph received two dreams about his future leadership.
- Even when he faced rejection, slavery, and prison, he held onto his dreams.
- Years later, those dreams came to pass.

Lesson: God can reveal your destiny in dreams before you are ready to walk in it.

<u>Dreams Are a Weapon in Spiritual Warfare</u>

As we explored in Chapter 13, dreams are not only divine messages—they are also battle strategies in spiritual warfare. God can use dreams to warn of the enemy's attacks, expose demonic strongholds, and equip intercessors for battle.

Example: Gideon's Victory Dream (Judges 7:13-15)

- Gideon overheard an enemy soldier describing a dream of their army being defeated.
- This revelation strengthened Gideon's faith, and he led Israel to victory.

Lesson: God uses dreams to equip believers for warfare and victory.

How to Continue Growing in Dream Interpretation

The journey of understanding and interpreting dreams does not stop here. Like any other spiritual gift, dream interpretation must be cultivated through practice, study, and the leading of the Holy Spirit.

<u>Keep a Lifelong Dream Journal</u>

Recording your dreams is not just a short-term exercise—it is a lifetime spiritual discipline.

- Keep writing down dreams.
- Review past dreams for patterns and fulfillment.
- Pray over your dreams and seek confirmation.

Many people discover that past dreams become clear years later, showing how God was speaking even when they did not recognize it at the time.

<u>Seek Ongoing Wisdom and Counsel</u>

- Surround yourself with mature believers who understand prophetic dreams.
- Continue studying Scripture to compare dreams with biblical patterns.
- Be humble and willing to learn—no one has perfect interpretation, and revelation unfolds over time.

"For we know in part and we prophesy in part." (1 Corinthians 13:9 NKJV)

Lesson: Dream interpretation is a journey, not a one-time event.

Increase Your Sensitivity to God's Voice

If you want to experience more prophetic dreams, cultivate an atmosphere where God's voice is welcome.

- Pray before sleep, inviting God to speak.
- Eliminate distractions that cloud your spiritual sensitivity.
- Live in purity—holiness increases clarity in the spirit realm.

"My sheep hear My voice, and I know them, and they follow Me." (John 10:27 NKJV)

Lesson: The more we value and respond to God's voice in dreams, the more He will entrust us with divine revelation.

The Responsibility of Stewarding Divine Revelation

Responding to Dreams With Obedience

When God speaks in a dream, it is not for entertainment—it is for action, prayer, or spiritual growth.

Example: Joseph Fleeing With Jesus (Matthew 2:13-15)

- Joseph was warned in a dream that Herod wanted to kill baby Jesus.
- He immediately obeyed and fled to Egypt, saving Jesus' life.

Lesson: Delayed obedience can lead to spiritual consequences.

<u>Praying Over Dreams Before Acting</u>

Not every dream should be acted on immediately. Some require:

- Prayer and discernment.
- Wise counsel from spiritual mentors.
- Waiting for God's timing.

"But Mary kept all these things and pondered them in her heart." (Luke 2:19 NKJV)

Lesson: Sometimes, God gives dreams that are meant to be hidden and prayed over until the right time.

<u>Sharing Dreams Wisely</u>

Not every dream is meant to be shared with everyone. Some are:

- Personal revelations for spiritual growth.
- Corporate warnings that require intercession.
- Prophetic confirmations that should be tested and weighed.

"Let two or three prophets speak, and let the others judge." (1 Corinthians 14:29 NKJV)

Lesson: Be led by the Holy Spirit when deciding when and with whom to share your dreams.

A Final Call to Awaken to the Supernatural Realm of Dreams

You were never meant to walk through life spiritually blind. God desires to speak to you, guide you, warn you, and reveal hidden things—and one of the primary ways He does this is through dreams. God is calling His people to:

- Recognize dreams as a vital part of their spiritual journey.
- Pursue deeper revelation through dream interpretation.
- Engage in spiritual warfare using dreams as weapons.
- Steward their dreams with prayer, wisdom, and obedience.

Now is the time to wake up to God's voice in the night. Are you listening?

Final Encouragement: A Prayer for Dream Revelation

If you desire to cultivate a lifestyle where God speaks to you in dreams, pray this:

"Heavenly Father, I thank You that You are always speaking. I open my heart and mind to hear Your voice in the night. Give me dreams that reveal Your plans, expose the enemy, and guide me in Your perfect will. Help me to discern, interpret, and respond to Your messages with wisdom and obedience. I dedicate my dream life to You, and I ask for greater clarity, insight, and spiritual sensitivity. In Jesus' name, amen."

Appendix 1: A Dream Dictionary of Common Biblical Symbols
Understanding Symbolism in Dreams

One of the greatest challenges in dream interpretation is understanding the symbolic language of the Spirit. God often speaks through images, metaphors, and parables in dreams, requiring spiritual discernment to uncover their meaning. Throughout the Bible, we see that God consistently used symbols in dreams and visions:

- Pharaoh's dream of cows and grain represented years of plenty and famine (Genesis 41).
- Nebuchadnezzar's dream of a great statue revealed the rise and fall of world empires (Daniel 2).
- Peter's vision of unclean animals symbolized the inclusion of Gentiles in the Church (Acts 10:9-16).

Dreams are rarely literal—they communicate spiritual truths through imagery that must be interpreted carefully. This appendix provides a biblical dream dictionary, offering common dream symbols and their possible meanings based on Scripture and prophetic patterns. However, keep in mind:

- Symbols can have different meanings depending on context.
- The Holy Spirit is the ultimate interpreter of dreams.
- Personal life experiences influence how certain symbols appear in dreams.

When interpreting a dream, always ask:

- What is the emotional tone of the dream?
- What does the Bible say about this symbol?
- Does this symbol have personal significance in my life?
- What is the Holy Spirit revealing?

Common Dream Symbols and Their Biblical Meanings

1. Water in Dreams

- Water often represents the Holy Spirit, life, cleansing, or spiritual condition.
- Clear, still water → Peace, Holy Spirit presence (John 7:38).
- Flowing rivers → Spiritual renewal, revival (Ezekiel 47:9).
- Stormy or muddy water → Confusion, spiritual warfare (Isaiah 57:20).
- Floods or rising water → Overwhelming circumstances, judgment (Genesis 6:17).

- Walking on water → Faith, overcoming obstacles (Matthew 14:29)

Understanding the Depth of Its Symbolism

Water is one of the most frequent and powerful symbols in dreams, representing spiritual life, cleansing, renewal, and movement. In the Bible, water is often associated with the Holy Spirit, purification, and divine provision, but it can also symbolize chaos, destruction, and overwhelming trials depending on its context in a dream.

Since water is essential for life, its presence in dreams often indicates a spiritual condition, emotional state, or divine intervention. The characteristics of the water—whether it is calm or stormy, clean or dirty, abundant or lacking—are key to understanding its meaning.

Below, we explore five major ways water appears in dreams and what they typically represent biblically and spiritually.

Clear, Still Water → Peace, Holy Spirit Presence

Clear, still water represents spiritual peace, the presence of God, and inner rest. It often indicates a season of calm, clarity, and divine refreshment. In John 7:38 NKJV, Jesus says:

"Whoever believes in Me, as Scripture has said, rivers of living water will flow from within them."

This verse confirms that water is a metaphor for the Holy Spirit's presence and activity in a believer's life. When you dream of still, clear water, it may signify:

- A deepening of your relationship with the Holy Spirit.
- A time of spiritual peace and rest in God's presence.
- A confirmation that you are walking in alignment with God's will.
- A season of healing and restoration.

Example Dream Interpretation

- If you dream of sitting beside a still lake, it may represent a time of deep inner peace, healing, and closeness with God.
- If you see yourself drinking clear water, it could symbolize that God is refreshing your soul with His Word and Spirit.

Your Response: Thank God for His presence, and use this time to draw closer to Him in prayer and worship.

Flowing Rivers → Spiritual Renewal, Revival

Flowing water, such as a river or stream, symbolizes movement, the work of the Holy Spirit, and spiritual life. It often represents revival, renewal, and God's refreshing power. In Ezekiel 47:9 NKJV, the prophet describes a vision of a river flowing from the temple, bringing life wherever it goes:

"Everything will live wherever the river goes."

A dream of flowing water can indicate:

- A season of spiritual growth and revival.
- A fresh move of the Holy Spirit in your life or church.
- An invitation to step deeper into God's calling and anointing.
- An outpouring of God's power and provision.

Example Dream Interpretation

- If you dream of standing in a flowing river, it could mean that God is leading you into a season of spiritual renewal.
- A raging river could indicate a powerful move of God that requires faith and trust to navigate.

Spiritual Response: Pray for a greater outpouring of the Holy Spirit and prepare to embrace the new things God is doing in your life.

<u>Stormy or Muddy Water</u> → <u>Confusion, Spiritual Warfare</u>

Unlike still water, stormy or muddy water often represents spiritual conflict, inner turmoil, or an attack from the enemy. Isaiah 57:20 NKJV warns:

"The wicked are like the troubled sea, when it cannot rest, whose waters cast up mire and dirt."

When water is muddy or stormy in a dream, it can indicate:

- A season of spiritual warfare, attacks, or opposition.

- Confusion, uncertainty, or emotional distress.
- A lack of spiritual clarity or discernment.
- The enemy trying to stir up chaos in your life.

Example Dream Interpretation

- If you dream of being caught in a stormy sea, it may mean you are facing spiritual battles and need to stand firm in faith.
- If you see muddy water covering your path, it could symbolize a lack of clarity about an important decision or situation.

Spiritual Response: Seek God for wisdom, engage in spiritual warfare through prayer, and ask for divine clarity to navigate through the situation.

Floods or Rising Water → Overwhelming Circumstances, Judgment

Floodwaters in dreams often symbolize overwhelming circumstances, spiritual attacks, or impending judgment. In Genesis 6:17, God warns of the flood that would cleanse the earth from sin:

"Behold, I will bring a flood of waters upon the earth, to destroy all flesh in which is the breath of life under heaven."

When water rises rapidly or floods a space, it may indicate:

- A season of overwhelming stress, trials, or testing.
- A warning dream about coming challenges.

- The need for prayer, repentance, or spiritual preparation.

Example Dream Interpretation

- If you dream of a flood destroying your home, it may indicate an area of your life where the enemy is attacking.
- If you see rising waters but you are standing on high ground, it could symbolize God's protection despite difficult circumstances.

Your Response: Seek God for protection, intercede for areas under attack, and stand firm in faith during trials.

Walking on Water → Faith, Overcoming Obstacles

Walking on water in a dream symbolizes faith, overcoming obstacles, and stepping into the supernatural. When Peter walked on water, Jesus said:

"Come," He said. Then Peter got down out of the boat, walked on the water, and came toward Jesus." (Matthew 14:29 NKJV)

If you dream of walking on water, it can mean:

- You are stepping out in faith into a new calling.
- God is inviting you into deeper spiritual experiences.
- You are overcoming fear and trusting in God's power.
- You are learning to walk by faith and not by sight.

Example Dream Interpretation

- If you dream of successfully walking on water, it may indicate you are growing in faith and trusting God more deeply.
- If you start sinking, it may represent doubt or struggles with trusting God in a difficult situation.

Your Response: If God is calling you to step out in faith, trust Him completely, and keep your eyes on Him, not on the waves around you.

Final Thoughts on Water in Dreams

Water is a powerful and multi-layered symbol in dreams. It can represent peace, the Holy Spirit, spiritual warfare, or overwhelming trials, depending on the condition of the water.

When interpreting a dream about water, always ask:

- Is the water clear or dirty?
- Is it peaceful or turbulent?
- What is my position in relation to the water?
- Does the dream bring peace or fear?

By praying for discernment and seeking biblical confirmation, you can unlock God's message through the prophetic language of water in dreams. Are you paying attention to the spiritual condition of the water in your dreams?

2. Fire in Dreams

Fire can signify God's presence, purification, or judgment.

- Burning bush → Divine calling (Exodus 3:2).
- Refining fire → Purification, testing (Malachi 3:2-3).
- Consuming fire → God's power, judgment (Hebrews 12:29).
- Fire destroying something → Spiritual attack, destruction.

Fire in Dreams: Understanding Its Prophetic Significance

Fire is one of the most powerful and multifaceted symbols in Scripture, carrying both positive and negative meanings depending on its context. In dreams, fire can signify:

- God's presence and power.
- Purification and refining.
- Judgment and destruction.
- Spiritual warfare and attacks from the enemy.

Fire is a force that transforms—it can purify gold, burn away impurities, provide light, or destroy whatever is in its path. Understanding the context, intensity, and impact of fire in a dream is key to interpreting its meaning. Below, we explore the four major ways fire appears in dreams and what they typically represent biblically and spiritually.

Burning Bush → Divine Calling

A burning bush represents a divine encounter, calling, or

commission from God. Unlike ordinary fire that consumes, the fire of the burning bush in Exodus 3 did not destroy—instead, it was a manifestation of God's presence and voice.

"The Angel of the LORD appeared to him in a flame of fire from within a bush. Moses saw that though the bush was on fire, it did not burn up." (*Exodus* 3:2 *NKJV*)

A dream of a burning bush or fire that does not consume may indicate:

- God is calling you into a new assignment or ministry.
- You are having a supernatural encounter that requires deeper attention.
- God's presence is manifesting in your life in a powerful way.
- You are standing on "holy ground," where divine revelation is unfolding.

Example Dream Interpretation

- If you dream of a bush on fire but not burning up, God may be revealing a divine purpose or calling for your life.
- If the fire speaks to you, as it did with Moses, pay attention to what is being said—it could be a direct message from God.

Your Response: Pray and ask God for confirmation. Seek wisdom on how to step into the calling being revealed.

Refining Fire → Purification, Testing

Fire often represents a refining process, where impurities are removed, and character is tested and strengthened. This type of fire is not meant to destroy but to purify and prepare.

"He will sit as a refiner and purifier of silver; He will purify the Levites and refine them like gold and silver. Then the LORD will have men who will bring offerings in righteousness."
(*Malachi* 3:3)

If you see a refining fire in a dream, it may indicate:

- You are going through a season of testing, growth, and purification.
- God is refining your faith, preparing you for greater things.
- There are areas in your life that God is burning away to bring forth purity.
- You are being prepared for ministry, leadership, or a new spiritual level.

Example Dream Interpretation

- If you dream of gold or silver being refined in fire, God may be purifying you through trials to bring out His character in you.
- If you see yourself walking through fire but not being burned, it may symbolize God sustaining you through a difficult season.

Your Response: Embrace God's refining work. Ask Him what areas of your life He is purifying and seek to align with His process.

Consuming Fire → God's Power, Judgment

God is often referred to as a consuming fire, signifying His holiness, power, and righteous judgment. Unlike refining fire that purifies, consuming fire destroys what is unholy or rebellious.

"For our God is a consuming fire." (*Hebrews* 12:29 *NKJV*)

In Scripture, fire was used as a sign of judgment against sin:

- Sodom and Gomorrah were destroyed by fire from heaven (Genesis 19:24).
- Nadab and Abihu were consumed by fire for offering strange incense (Leviticus 10:1-2).
- Elijah called down fire to demonstrate God's power over false gods (1 Kings 18:38).

If you dream of a consuming fire, it may indicate:

- God is bringing judgment against sin or injustice.
- A cleansing and removal of wickedness is taking place.
- You are experiencing the overwhelming presence of God's power.
- Spiritual strongholds or demonic influences are being burned away.

Example Dream Interpretation

- If you see a city or nation consumed by fire, it may represent judgment, transformation, or a call to intercession for that place.

- If fire from heaven falls on an altar, it could symbolize God's approval, power, or a fresh outpouring of His Spirit.

Your Response: If the dream carries a warning, seek God in prayer and intercede for those involved. If it represents God's power, seek Him for deeper encounters.

Fire Destroying Something → Spiritual Attack, Destruction

While fire can be a sign of God's presence or purification, it can also represent destruction, loss, and attacks from the enemy.

- The enemy often uses fire to symbolize devastation, loss, and chaos (John 10:10).
- Fire destroying homes, churches, or relationships in dreams may indicate spiritual attacks or loss.
- Uncontrolled fire can signify anger, judgment, or strongholds that need breaking.

A dream of fire destroying something valuable may indicate:

- A spiritual attack against your family, finances, or faith.
- A warning to pray against demonic schemes meant to bring destruction.
- An area of your life that is under attack and needs protection.
- A call to intercede for a church, ministry, or nation experiencing opposition.

Example Dream Interpretation

- If you dream of your home burning down, it may symbolize spiritual warfare in your household.
- If you see your workplace or church on fire, it may be a call to pray against attacks or division in that place.
- If fire is consuming everything around you but not harming you, it may mean God is removing things from your life that are not aligned with His will.

Your Response: Pray against spiritual attacks. Ask God for discernment, protection, and wisdom in how to respond.

<u>Final Thoughts on Fire in Dreams</u>

Fire is a powerful and deeply spiritual symbol that can indicate:

- God's calling and presence (Burning Bush)
- Spiritual growth and purification (Refining Fire)
- God's power and righteous judgment (Consuming Fire)
- Spiritual attacks, destruction, or demonic schemes (Destructive Fire)

Questions to Ask When Interpreting Fire in Dreams:

- Is the fire bringing purification or destruction?
- Is the fire a manifestation of God's presence or a warning of judgment?
- Am I being refined, called, or warned?

- How do I feel in the dream—peaceful, afraid, or empowered?

Fire is not to be feared but understood. It can be a sign of God's power, a process of purification, or a call to intercede against destruction. Are you discerning the message behind the fire in your dreams?

3. Trees in Dreams

Trees symbolize spiritual growth, nations, or individuals.

- A flourishing tree → Fruitfulness, divine favor (Psalm 1:3).
- A tree being cut down → Judgment, transition (Daniel 4:14).
- A tree with deep roots → Spiritual stability (Jeremiah 17:8).
- A dead or barren tree → Lack of spiritual growth, curse (Matthew 21:19).

Trees in Dreams: Understanding Their Spiritual Symbolism

Trees are powerful symbols in dreams, often representing spiritual growth, individuals, nations, stability, or divine judgment. Trees are living, growing, and deeply rooted, making them a strong biblical metaphor for both life and death, prosperity and destruction.

In Scripture, trees appear frequently to represent righteousness, fruitfulness, seasons of change, and even divine warnings. Psalm 1:3 compares the righteous believer to a tree planted by streams of water, while in Daniel 4, a tree symbolizes Nebuchadnezzar's kingdom, which was cut down as an act of divine judgment.

When interpreting a dream about trees, consider:

- The type of tree (flourishing, barren, uprooted, etc.).
- The location (planted by water, in a dry place, cut down, etc.).
- The condition of the tree (healthy, dead, bearing fruit, etc.).

A Flourishing Tree → Fruitfulness, Divine Favor

A flourishing tree represents spiritual health, stability, and divine favor. In Psalm 1:3 (NKJV), the righteous are described as:

"He is like a tree planted by streams of water, that yields its fruit in its season, and its leaf does not wither. In all that he does, he prospers."

If you dream of a strong, healthy tree, it may symbolize:

- Spiritual growth and maturity.
- Being deeply rooted in Christ and His Word.
- Bearing spiritual fruit—love, joy, peace, etc. (Galatians 5:22-23).
- A season of divine favor and prosperity.

Example Dream Interpretation

- If you see yourself sitting under a large, fruitful tree, it may indicate that you are in a season of stability and spiritual nourishment.
- If you dream of planting a tree, it could symbolize the beginning of a spiritual journey or ministry that will grow over time.

Your Response: Give thanks to God for your growth and ask for continued strength and fruitfulness.

A Tree Being Cut Down → Judgment, Transition

A tree being cut down in a dream often signifies judgment, a major transition, or the removal of something significant. In Daniel 4:14 NKJV, Nebuchadnezzar received a dream of a massive tree being cut down, which represented the loss of his kingdom due to his pride:

"Cut down the tree and lop off its branches, strip off its leaves and scatter its fruit!"

If you dream of a tree being cut down, it may symbolize:

- A warning about pride, sin, or impending consequences.
- The end of a season, ministry, or relationship.
- Divine pruning—God removing things that no longer serve His purpose.
- A call to repentance before judgment falls.

Example Dream Interpretation

- If you dream of a strong tree being cut down, it may indicate a shift or loss in authority, position, or influence.
- If you see yourself cutting down a tree, it could symbolize a personal decision to remove something unhealthy from your life.

Your Response: Pray for discernment—if the dream is a warning, seek repentance and alignment with God's will.

A Tree With Deep Roots → Spiritual Stability

A tree with deep roots represents spiritual depth, faithfulness, and the ability to endure trials.

"He is like a tree planted by water, that sends out its roots by the stream, and does not fear when heat comes, for its leaves remain green, and it is not anxious in the year of drought, for it does not cease to bear fruit." (Jeremiah 17:8 NKJV)

If you dream of a tree with deep, strong roots, it may symbolize:

- A firm foundation in Christ and the Word of God.
- The ability to withstand trials and adversity.
- A call to deepen your spiritual roots in prayer and study.
- Security and confidence in God's provision.

Example Dream Interpretation

- If you see yourself planting a tree and its roots going deep into the ground, it may indicate a call to spiritual growth and grounding yourself in God's Word.

- If you see a tree swaying in the wind but not breaking, it could symbolize resilience through trials.

Your Response: Strengthen your foundation in Christ through prayer, fasting, and studying Scripture.

A Dead or Barren Tree → Lack of Spiritual Growth, Curse

A dead or barren tree often represents a lack of fruitfulness, spiritual stagnation, or even divine judgment. In Matthew 21:19, Jesus cursed a fig tree that bore no fruit, saying:

"May you never bear fruit again!" Immediately the tree withered."

If you dream of a dead or barren tree, it may symbolize:

- Spiritual dryness or lack of growth.
- Unproductive areas of life or ministry.
- A warning to return to faithfulness and fruit-bearing.
- A need for revival and restoration.

Example Dream Interpretation

- If you see a tree that once bore fruit but is now withered, it could be a warning about spiritual neglect.

- If you try to revive a dead tree in your dream, it
  may symbolize a call to rekindle your passion
  for God.

Your Response: Ask the Holy Spirit to reveal any areas of
spiritual dryness and seek renewal through worship, prayer,
and repentance.

4. Animals in Dreams

Animals often represent spiritual forces, personal characteristics, or nations. Animals in Dreams: Understanding Their
Spiritual Significance Animals in dreams often carry deep
prophetic meanings and can symbolize:

- Spiritual forces—both divine and demonic.
- Personal characteristics—strength, deception,
  wisdom, or aggression.
- Nations, leaders, or prophetic messages—just as in
  biblical prophecy.

Throughout Scripture, animals are frequently used to
symbolize spiritual realities:

- The Holy Spirit descended like a dove at Jesus'
  baptism (Matthew 3:16).
- The devil is described as a serpent and a roaring
  lion (Genesis 3:1, 1 Peter 5:8).
- The four beasts in Daniel's vision represented
  world empires (Daniel 7:1-8).

When interpreting an animal dream, ask:

- What kind of animal is it? (Peaceful, aggressive, wild, or tame?)
- What is the animal doing? (Attacking, guiding, speaking, hiding?)
- How does the dream make you feel? (Fear, peace, joy, urgency?)

This section explores the biblical meanings of animals in dreams, divided into positive and negative symbols.

Positive Animals in Dreams

Some animals carry positive spiritual meanings, representing God's nature, divine protection, prophetic insight, and strength.

Dove → Holy Spirit, Peace

The dove is a universal symbol of peace, purity, and the presence of the Holy Spirit. In Matthew 3:16 NKJV, when Jesus was baptized:

"The heavens were opened to Him, and He saw the Spirit of God descending like a dove and alighting upon Him."

If you dream of a dove, it may symbolize:

- The presence of the Holy Spirit in your life.
- God's guidance, peace, or a fresh spiritual renewal.
- A call to walk in gentleness, purity, and obedience.
- A confirmation of God's favor and blessing over your decisions.

Example Dream Interpretation

- If you see a dove landing on your shoulder, it may mean God is confirming His presence and calling over your life.
- If a dove flies toward you in a dream, it may indicate a season of peace or the Holy Spirit leading you into something new.

Your Response: Invite the Holy Spirit to speak, pray for clarity, and move forward with peace in your decisions.

Eagle → Spiritual Vision, Prophetic Calling

The eagle represents spiritual strength, prophetic vision, and divine elevation. Isaiah 40:31 NKJV declares:

"But those who wait on the Lord shall renew their strength; they shall mount up with wings like eagles."

If you dream of an eagle, it may signify:

- God is calling you into a prophetic or leadership role.
- A new season of heightened spiritual vision and discernment.
- Strength to overcome obstacles through God's power.
- A calling to higher realms of faith, wisdom, and spiritual insight.

Example Dream Interpretation

- If you dream of flying with eagles, it could mean God is elevating you into a new level of authority and wisdom.
- If an eagle lands near you, it may be a sign of prophetic insight coming your way.

Your Response: Pray for clarity regarding your spiritual calling and seek to grow in wisdom and discernment.

Lamb → Innocence, Jesus Christ

The lamb represents purity, sacrifice, and the person of Jesus Christ. John 1:29 NKJV declares:

"Behold, the Lamb of God who takes away the sin of the world!"

If you dream of a lamb, it may indicate:

- God is calling you to a place of innocence, surrender, and humility.
- A reminder of Jesus' sacrifice and redemption for you.
- A season of deep intimacy with God, free from distractions.
- An invitation to live in purity and holiness.

Example Dream Interpretation

- If you hold a lamb in your dream, it may represent God's call to a place of spiritual purity and trust in Him.
- If a lamb is following you, it could indicate a calling to shepherd and lead others in faith.

Your Response: Draw closer to Jesus, embrace humility, and seek to live a holy life before God.

<u>Lion → Jesus as the Lion of Judah</u>

The lion represents authority, boldness, and the kingship of Jesus Christ. In Revelation 5:5 NKJV, Jesus is called:

> *"The Lion of the tribe of Judah, the Root of David, has prevailed."*

If you dream of a lion, it may signify:

- Spiritual strength, courage, and dominion in your calling.
- Jesus fighting on your behalf, bringing victory over enemies.
- A call to step into leadership or confront spiritual battles boldly.
- A season of breakthrough, where you are rising in spiritual authority.

Example Dream Interpretation

- If you see a lion roaring, it may indicate boldness and victory in your spiritual life.
- If you ride on a lion's back, it may symbolize God carrying you into a place of spiritual authority.

Your Response: Embrace courage, stand firm in spiritual battles, and walk in divine authority.

<u>Negative Animals in Dreams</u>

Some animals symbolize demonic forces, deception, or spiritual attacks.

Snake → Satan, Deception

Snakes represent deception, temptation, or demonic activity. In Genesis 3:1 NKJV, the devil appeared as a serpent to deceive Eve. If you see a snake in a dream, it may indicate:

- Spiritual deception or false teachings.
- A person in your life who is not trustworthy.
- A warning about temptation or hidden sin.
- The enemy trying to infiltrate your thoughts or decisions.

Your Response: Pray for discernment, rebuke deception, and seek wisdom in your relationships and decisions.

Wolf → False Teachers, Danger

Jesus warned about wolves in sheep's clothing in Matthew 7:15 NKJV:

"Beware of false prophets, who come to you in sheep's clothing but inwardly are ravenous wolves."

If you see a wolf in a dream, it may indicate:

- A person or leader with deceptive intentions.
- A warning against false doctrine or manipulation.
- A spiritual attack that requires prayer and discernment.

Your Response: Pray for protection, stay grounded in biblical truth, and avoid being led astray.

<u>Scorpion</u> → <u>Demonic Attack</u>

Scorpions are symbols of demonic attacks, affliction, and danger. Jesus said in Luke 10:19 NKJV:

> *"Behold, I give you the authority to trample on serpents and scorpions, and over all the power of the enemy."*

If you dream of a scorpion, it may indicate:

- Spiritual warfare and demonic oppression.
- An attack against your mind, body, or emotions.
- The enemy trying to cause harm or distraction.

Your Response: Use spiritual authority in prayer to rebuke the enemy and walk in victory.

5. Numbers in Dreams

Numbers in dreams are often prophetic messages from God, carrying deep biblical significance. In Scripture, numbers frequently symbolize spiritual truths, divine patterns, and prophetic meanings. For example:

- Pharaoh's dream of seven years of plenty followed by seven years of famine (Genesis 41:25-32) confirmed God's divine plan.
- Daniel's prophetic visions used numbers to reveal the timing of events in God's plan for Israel (Daniel 9:24-27).

- Jesus fasted for 40 days in the wilderness,
  symbolizing a period of testing and preparation
  (Matthew 4:2).

When you repeatedly see a certain number in a
dream, it is important to pray and seek understanding
about what God may be communicating. This section
explores the prophetic meaning of numbers in dreams,
focusing on five significant biblical numbers and their
implications.

Number 1 → Unity, New Beginnings

The number 1 in dreams represents unity, new beginnings,
leadership, and God's sovereignty. It often signifies a fresh start,
divine alignment, or the oneness of God.

- God's Oneness: "Hear, O Israel: The Lord our
  God, the Lord is one!" (Deuteronomy 6:4)
- New Beginnings: "In the beginning, God created
  the heavens and the earth." (Genesis 1:1)
- First Fruits & Leadership: The firstborn in
  Scripture often symbolized inheritance and
  authority.

Possible Dream Interpretations

If you dream of the number 1, it may indicate:

- A new chapter in your life, ministry, or spiritual
  walk.
- God calling you into leadership or greater
  responsibility.

- A reminder to focus on God as your primary source.

If you see yourself standing alone in a dream, it may mean God is setting you apart for a special purpose. Your Response: Seek God for clarity on the new beginning He is leading you into.

Number 3 → The Trinity, Divine Completeness

The number 3 represents divine wholeness, the Trinity (Father, Son, Holy Spirit), and resurrection power.

- The Trinity: "Go therefore and make disciples of all nations, baptizing them in the name of the Father and the Son and the Holy Spirit." (Matthew 28:19)
- Resurrection Power: Jesus rose from the dead on the third day (Luke 24:7).
- Divine Order: Many things in Scripture occur in groups of three—faith, hope, love (1 Corinthians 13:13).

Possible Dream Interpretations

If you dream of the number 3, it may signify:

- A divine alignment with God's will.
- A resurrection or revival in an area of your life.
- A call to deeper intimacy with the Father, Son, and Holy Spirit.

If you see three doors, three steps, or three candles, it may indicate a process of spiritual growth or preparation for something new. Your Response: Seek to grow in your relationship with God and be open to a season of transformation.

Number 7 → Perfection, Completion

The number 7 is one of the most significant prophetic numbers in the Bible, representing perfection, completion, and divine rest.

- God's Creation: "On the seventh day God finished His work that He had done, and He rested on the seventh day." (Genesis 2:2)
- Spiritual Perfection: The number 7 appears hundreds of times in Scripture, signifying God's perfect work.
- Prophetic Cycles: The Book of Revelation is filled with seven churches, seven seals, seven trumpets, and seven bowls of judgment.

Possible Dream Interpretations

If you keep seeing the number 7 in dreams, it may indicate:

- The completion of a season in your life.
- A confirmation that God's work in an area is finished.
- A time of divine rest and spiritual perfection.

If you dream of seven candles, seven people, or seven doors, it may signify God bringing completion to a certain area in your life. Your Response: Ask God if He is leading you into a season of completion, breakthrough, or rest.

Number 12 → Government, Apostolic Authority

The number 12 represents divine government, apostolic authority, and perfect order.

- 12 Tribes of Israel: God established 12 tribes to govern Israel (Genesis 49:28).
- 12 Apostles: Jesus appointed 12 apostles to lay the foundation of the Church (Matthew 10:2-4).
- Heavenly Order: The New Jerusalem has 12 gates, 12 foundations, and 12 angels (Revelation 21:12-14).

Possible Dream Interpretations

If you dream of the number 12, it may indicate:

- A call to leadership or spiritual authority.
- Divine structure or government being established in your life.
- A season of apostolic commissioning or discipleship.

If you see 12 chairs, 12 steps, or 12 keys, it may represent a foundational role in a spiritual assignment. Your Response: Seek God for wisdom on how to walk in divine order and spiritual leadership.

Number 40 → A Time of Testing or Transition

The number 40 is consistently used in Scripture to represent a season of testing, trial, and transition.

- 40 Days of Flood: Noah endured 40 days and nights of rain (Genesis 7:12).
- 40 Years in the Wilderness: Israel wandered 40 years before entering the Promised Land (Deuteronomy 8:2).
- 40 Days of Fasting: Jesus fasted 40 days before beginning His ministry (Matthew 4:2).

Possible Dream Interpretations

If you dream of the number 40, it may signify:

- A season of testing or spiritual refinement.
- A transition into a new chapter after endurance.
- A need for perseverance and preparation.

If you see 40 steps, 40 doors, or 40 days on a calendar, it may indicate a period of spiritual testing that will soon end. Your Response: Trust that God is preparing you for something greater through the trial you are facing.

How to Discern and Respond to Numbers in Dreams

Step 1: Pray for Revelation

Numbers in dreams are not coincidences—they carry prophetic weight. Ask the Holy Spirit:
"Lord, what are You speaking to me through this number?"

Step 2: Compare With Scripture

Look for biblical patterns of how the number is used. If the number aligns with a biblical meaning, it is likely a message from God.

Step 3: Look for Repeated Occurrences

If a number appears repeatedly in different dreams, it is a confirmation that God is emphasizing something important.

Step 4: Seek Wise Counsel

If you are unsure about the meaning of a number in your dream, seek spiritual mentors or prophetic leaders who can help interpret it biblically.

Final Thoughts on Numbers in Dreams

Numbers are one of God's prophetic languages, used to confirm, direct, and prepare His people.

- Pay attention to recurring numbers in dreams.
- Compare numbers with biblical patterns and meanings.
- Pray for wisdom and discernment in responding to what God is revealing.

Are you noticing a pattern of numbers in your dreams? If so, God may be trying to speak something significant to you!

7. Houses and Buildings in Dreams

Houses and buildings in dreams often represent a person's life, spiritual condition, or family. They can also symbolize:

- Your inner life—your heart, mind, and soul.
- Your family, household, or generational patterns.
- A church, ministry, or spiritual calling.
- Opportunities, transitions, or limitations.

Throughout Scripture, houses and buildings are frequently used as metaphors:

- Jesus compared a person's life to a house built on either rock or sand (Matthew 7:24-27).
- Paul described believers as temples of the Holy Spirit (1 Corinthians 6:19).
- Jesus spoke of many rooms in His Father's house, symbolizing spiritual capacity and eternal dwelling (John 14:2).

When interpreting a dream about a house, consider:

- The condition of the house (new, old, clean, broken, under construction).
- The location (by water, on a hill, in a dangerous area).
- Your actions (entering, leaving, repairing, discovering rooms).
- Who is present in the house (family, strangers, enemies).

This section explores common house and building symbols in dreams, with their biblical significance and practical interpretation.

A Well-Kept House → Spiritual Health, Stability

A well-kept, strong, and clean house represents spiritual stability, wisdom, and a well-established life. Jesus said:

"Everyone who hears these words of Mine and does them will be like a wise man who built his house on the rock." (Matthew 7:24 NKJV)

A well-kept house in a dream may indicate:

- A strong spiritual foundation rooted in Christ.
- A season of stability, peace, and divine order.
- That you are spiritually healthy and walking in wisdom.

Example Dream Interpretation

- If you dream of a well-maintained house, it could symbolize that your faith is strong, and you are in alignment with God's will.
- If you clean a house in your dream, it may indicate a season of purification, repentance, and renewal.

Your Response: Give thanks for spiritual stability and continue strengthening your walk with God.

A Broken-Down House → Spiritual Neglect, Strongholds

A damaged, abandoned, or broken-down house can symbolize spiritual neglect, sin, or demonic strongholds. Proverbs 24:30-31 NKJV warns:

"I went past the field of a sluggard, past the vineyard of someone who has no sense; thorns had come up everywhere, the ground was covered with weeds, and the stone wall was in ruins."

A broken-down house in a dream may indicate:

- Spiritual neglect—lack of prayer, worship, or time in the Word.
- Demonic strongholds—unaddressed sin, oppression, or generational bondage.
- A broken foundation—an unstable spiritual or emotional life.
- A call to restore what has been abandoned or neglected.

Example Dream Interpretation

- If you enter a house with broken walls and holes in the roof, it may symbolize spiritual vulnerability and open doors to the enemy.
- If you try to repair an old house, it could mean God is calling you to restore neglected spiritual areas or broken relationships.

Your Response: Repent of any spiritual neglect, seek deliverance if necessary, and rebuild your faith through prayer and the Word.

A House With Many Rooms → Expanding Spiritual Capacity

A house with many rooms represents growth, expansion, new opportunities, and deeper spiritual capacity. Jesus said:

"In My Father's house are many rooms; if it were not so, would I have told you that I go to prepare a place for you?" (John 14:2 NKJV)

A house with many rooms in a dream may indicate:

- Spiritual promotion—God is expanding your understanding, influence, or anointing.
- New opportunities—new ministry, job, or relationships.
- A deeper understanding of God's mysteries—He is revealing more to you.
- Exploring different areas of your soul—God is working on multiple aspects of your life.

Example Dream Interpretation

- If you discover a new room in a house, it may mean God is unlocking new spiritual gifts, callings, or opportunities in your life.
- If the rooms are beautifully furnished, it may indicate blessings, preparation, or areas of your life that are thriving.

Your Response: Be open to spiritual growth, embrace new opportunities, and seek God for wisdom in expanding your influence.

A Locked Door in a House → Hindrances, Missed Opportunities

Doors in dreams often symbolize access, transition, and opportunities. A locked or closed door can indicate hindrances, missed opportunities, or something being hidden from you. Jesus said:

> *"I have set before you an open door, which no one is able to shut."* (Revelation 3:8 NKJV)

A locked door in a house in a dream may indicate:

- Spiritual blockages—something preventing you from stepping into your calling.
- Unforgiveness or emotional barriers—locked doors can symbolize areas of your heart that are shut off.
- Missed opportunities—you may need to ask God for another chance.
- Hidden revelation—God may be calling you to seek deeper understanding.

Example Dream Interpretation

- If you try to open a locked door but cannot, it may mean there is something blocking your progress spiritually or physically.
- If a key appears in your dream, it may indicate God giving you access to something previously closed off.

Your Response: Ask God for wisdom on whether to persist in seeking an opportunity or to trust His timing if a door remains closed.

Other House and Building Symbols in Dreams

Moving to a New House → A New Season or Transition

If you dream of moving into a new house, it may indicate:

- A new spiritual season—growth, transformation, or change.
- Leaving the past behind—God is bringing you into something new.
- A shift in your spiritual identity or calling.

An Abandoned House → Neglect, Unresolved Issues

If you dream of walking into an abandoned house, it may mean:

- Unfinished business—old wounds, forgotten promises, or unrepented sin.
- A need to return to something God once spoke over your life.

A Large Building or Mansion → Spiritual Authority or Kingdom Influence

If you see yourself in a massive building, it may symbolize:

- God expanding your influence.
- A new level of anointing, wisdom, or responsibility.

How to Interpret and Respond to House Dreams

Step 1: Identify the House's Condition

- Is it well-kept or broken?
- Is it new, old, or abandoned?

Step 2: Pay Attention to the Doors, Windows, and Rooms

- Are there open doors or locked doors?
- Are you discovering new rooms, or are certain areas restricted?

Step 3: Look for Who Is Inside the House

- Are you alone, or are others with you?
- Are there familiar people or strangers?

Step 4: Pray for Revelation and Guidance

- Ask God what the house represents—your spiritual life, family, or something else?
- If the house is in poor condition, ask how to restore it.
- If the house is beautiful, ask how to maintain and steward what God is giving you

Final Thoughts on Houses in Dreams

Houses are one of the most personal and powerful symbols in dreams, often revealing your spiritual state, family dynamics, or divine transitions.

- Pay attention to the house's condition, doors, and rooms.
- Ask the Holy Spirit to reveal what the dream means.
- Respond in prayer—whether to embrace, restore, or prepare for change.

What does your house dream reveal about your spiritual life?

Roads and Paths in Dreams: Understanding Their Spiritual Significance

Roads and paths in dreams often symbolize life's journey, spiritual direction, and the decisions we face. They reveal where we are going, how we are progressing, and whether we are aligned with God's will. In the Bible, roads, paths, and ways frequently represent:

- Spiritual direction ("The steps of a good man are ordered by the Lord." – Psalm 37:23 NKJV).
- God's guidance and leading ("I will instruct you and teach you in the way you should go." – Psalm 32:8 NKJV).
- Obedience or disobedience ("There is a way that seems right to a man, but its end is the way of death." – Proverbs 14:12 NKJV).
- The journey of faith ("Enter through the narrow gate, for wide is the gate and broad is the road that leads to destruction." – Matthew 7:13-14 NKJV).

When interpreting a dream about roads and paths, consider:

- The condition of the road (straight, winding, blocked, broken, etc.).
- Where the road leads (a city, a dead end, a mountain, etc.).
- Your movement (walking, running, struggling, following someone, etc.).

- What is happening on the road (traffic, roadblocks, people, detours, etc.).

This section explores the most common road and path symbols in dreams, their biblical significance, and how to respond.

<u>A Straight Road</u> → <u>Walking in God's Will</u>

A straight road represents God's divine direction, clarity, and obedience to His will.

"In all your ways acknowledge Him, and He will make your paths straight." (Proverbs 3:6 NKJV)

If you dream of a straight and clear road, it may symbolize:

- Walking in alignment with God's plan for your life.
- A season of clarity and divine favor.
- Obedience and spiritual discipline.
- A smooth journey ahead with little resistance.

Example Dream Interpretation

- If you dream of walking on a straight road toward a bright destination, it may indicate God is leading you into a season of purpose and clarity.
- If the road is illuminated or peaceful, it could signify confirmation that you are following God's will.

Your Response: Continue seeking God in prayer and stay faithful in your current direction.

A Fork in the Road → A Decision That Needs to Be Made

A fork in the road symbolizes a major life decision or crossroads in your spiritual journey:

"Thus says the Lord: 'Stand in the ways and see, and ask for the old paths, where the good way is, and walk in it; then you will find rest for your souls.'" (Jeremiah 6:16 NKJV)

If you dream of a fork in the road, it may indicate:

- A choice between two paths, ministries, or life directions.
- A spiritual test requiring wisdom and discernment.
- God presenting you with options—one leading to righteousness, the other leading to compromise.
- A moment where prayer and godly counsel are needed.

Example Dream Interpretation

- If you see two roads, one dark and one bright, it may symbolize the choice between good and evil or obedience and rebellion.
- If one road is smooth and the other is rocky, it may indicate one path is easy but leads to destruction, while the harder path leads to spiritual growth.

Your Response: Ask God for wisdom and discernment before making any major decisions. Seek confirmation through Scripture and godly counsel.

A Narrow Path → The Way of Righteousness

A narrow path represents a life of holiness, faithfulness, and obedience to God's commands.

"But small is the gate and narrow the road that leads to life, and only a few find it." (Matthew 7:14 NKJV)

If you dream of walking on a narrow path, it may signify:

- God is calling you to a life of purity and dedication.
- You are on the right path, even if it feels lonely or difficult.
- A reminder to stay committed to truth, even when pressured to compromise.
- A refining season where God is deepening your faith and character.

Example Dream Interpretation

- If you see yourself walking on a narrow but well-lit path, it may indicate God is leading you in righteousness despite opposition.
- If the path is difficult but you feel peace, it may symbolize spiritual growth through trials.

Your Response: Stay faithful, seek God's strength, and do not be discouraged if the journey feels hard.

A Detour or Roadblock → Delays, Spiritual Obstacles

A detour or blocked road represents delays, spiritual obstacles, or divine redirection.

"Many are the plans in a person's heart, but it is the Lord's purpose that prevails." (*Proverbs 19:21 NKJV*)

If you dream of a detour or roadblock, it may indicate:

- A delay in plans—God is redirecting you to something better.
- An obstacle in your spiritual journey that requires breakthrough prayer.
- A season where patience and trust in God are necessary.
- A warning to check if you are going in the wrong direction.

Example Dream Interpretation

- If you see a roadblock preventing you from moving forward, it may symbolize spiritual warfare, opposition, or a need for prayer and perseverance.
- If you take a detour and find a better road, it may indicate God is leading you in a different direction for His greater purpose.

Your Response: Seek God for clarity—if He is closing a door, trust that He has a better way prepared for you.

Other Road and Path Symbols in Dreams

Running on a Road → Acceleration or Rushing Ahead

If you dream of running on a road, it may indicate:

- A season of acceleration—God is fast-tracking your spiritual growth.
- Moving too fast without seeking God's timing.

<u>Traffic Jams → Delays and Frustration</u>

If you dream of being stuck in traffic, it may symbolize:

- Spiritual stagnation—something is hindering your progress.
- A need to slow down and wait for God's perfect timing.

<u>A Bridge on the Road → Transition and Faith</u>

If you dream of crossing a bridge, it may mean:

- A transition from one season to another.
- A faith test—trusting God to bring you safely across.

<u>A Road Leading to a Mountain → Spiritual Promotion</u>

If your road leads up a mountain, it may signify:

- God is calling you to higher spiritual levels.
- A season of breakthrough and overcoming challenges.

<u>How to Interpret and Respond to Road Dreams</u>

<u>Step 1: Identify the Condition of the Road</u>

- Is it straight, winding, blocked, or broken?
- Is it easy to walk on or full of obstacles?

Step 2: Pay Attention to Your Actions

- Are you walking, running, driving, or struggling?
- Are you choosing a path or facing a dead end?

Step 3: Seek God's Direction

- Is this dream revealing a decision you must make?
- Is God calling you to trust Him despite delays?
- Are you on the right spiritual path?

Final Thoughts on Roads in Dreams

Roads symbolize life's journey, spiritual progress, and divine direction.

- Pay attention to road conditions and obstacles.
- Ask the Holy Spirit for wisdom and discernment.
- Trust that God is leading you, even when the way seems unclear.

Are you walking on the path God has prepared for you?

8. Weapons in Dreams

Weapons in dreams are powerful symbols of spiritual warfare, divine authority, protection, and readiness for battle. Throughout the Bible, weapons are used both figuratively and literally to describe:

- The Word of God as a weapon against the enemy (Ephesians 6:17).
- Faith as a shield against spiritual attacks (Ephesians 6:16).
- Arrows as weapons used by both the enemy and God (Psalm 91:5).
- Armor as preparation for spiritual battles (Ephesians 6:11).

When interpreting dreams about weapons, consider:

- Who is holding the weapon? (Is it you, an angel, or an enemy?)
- What is the weapon used for? (Attack, defense, empowerment, or destruction?)
- How do you feel in the dream? (Fearful, empowered, victorious, or weak?)

This section explores the most common weapon symbols in dreams, their biblical significance, and how to interpret and respond to them.

Sword → The Word of God

The sword represents the Word of God, truth, and spiritual authority.

"Take the helmet of salvation and the sword of the Spirit, which is the Word of God." (Ephesians 6:17 NKJV)

A sword in a dream may symbolize:

- Spiritual authority to fight the enemy.

- Victory over lies and deception through God's truth.
- An ability to cut through confusion and bring clarity.
- A divine call to wield Scripture in warfare and prayer.

Example Dream Interpretation

- If you hold a shining sword, it may mean God has equipped you with His Word to fight spiritual battles.
- If you see a sword striking down an enemy, it could symbolize the power of God's truth defeating lies or spiritual attacks.
- If someone hands you a sword, it may indicate a divine commissioning or new level of spiritual responsibility.

Your Response: Strengthen your knowledge of Scripture, use the Word in prayer, and stand firm in spiritual warfare.

Shield → Faith, Protection

The shield represents faith, divine protection, and the ability to resist enemy attacks.

"Above all, taking the shield of faith, with which you will be able to quench all the fiery darts of the wicked one." (Ephesians 6:16 NKJV)

A shield in a dream may symbolize:

- Spiritual protection from the enemy's attacks.
- A call to strengthen your faith and trust in God.
- The ability to deflect lies, doubt, and fear.
- A defense against demonic oppression or accusations.

Example Dream Interpretation

- If you dream of holding a strong, unbreakable shield, it may indicate your faith is protecting you from spiritual attacks.
- If your shield is cracked or weak, it could mean you need to strengthen your faith and trust in God's promises.
- If an angel gives you a shield, it may symbolize divine protection being granted to you in a specific area of life.

Your Response: Pray for increased faith, declare God's promises over your life, and trust that He is your protector.

<u>Armor</u> → <u>Spiritual Preparedness</u>

Armor in dreams represents spiritual readiness, divine protection, and preparation for battle.

"Put on the whole armor of God, that you may be able to stand against the schemes of the devil." (Ephesians 6:11 NKJV)

Armor in a dream may symbolize:

- God equipping you for spiritual warfare.

- A need to be vigilant and prepared for battles ahead.
- The importance of staying clothed in righteousness and truth.
- A divine calling to intercede and stand firm in faith.

Example Dream Interpretation

- If you see yourself fully armored, it may indicate you are spiritually prepared for what's ahead.
- If your armor is damaged, it may mean the enemy has found a weak spot in your spiritual life.
- If you are missing a piece of armor (e.g., no helmet or shield), it may suggest you need to focus on strengthening that area—whether it's salvation, faith, truth, or righteousness.

Your Response: Assess your spiritual readiness, pray for strength, and ensure you are fully armored in God's protection.

Arrows → Spiritual Attacks or Assignments

Arrows in dreams can symbolize both attacks from the enemy and divine assignments sent by God.

"You shall not be afraid of the terror by night, nor of the arrow that flies by day." (Psalm 91:5 NKJV)

Arrows in a dream may symbolize:

- Spiritual warfare—an enemy attack against your mind, health, or destiny.

- Words—spoken accusations, curses, or negative declarations.
- God's divine assignments or messages being released.
- A call to prayer and intercession to block enemy attacks.

Example Dream Interpretation

- If you dream of arrows being shot at you, it may indicate spiritual warfare and the need for prayer and protection.
- If you shoot an arrow at a target, it may symbolize God giving you a specific assignment or mission.
- If an arrow is stuck in your body, it may indicate a past wound or attack that needs healing

Response: Break every demonic attack in prayer, declare God's protection, and seek wisdom on any assignments He is giving you.

Other Weapons and Their Meanings in Dreams

Two-Edged Sword → Judgment, Power of the Word

"For the Word of God is alive and active. Sharper than any double-edged sword." (Hebrews 4:12 NKJV)

If you dream of a two-edged sword, it may indicate a powerful anointing in declaring God's Word and bringing truth to others.

Golden Shield → Divine Protection, Honor

"You, O Lord, are a shield around me, my glory, and the One who lifts my head." (Psalm 3:3 NKJV)

A golden shield may symbolize divine favor and supernatural protection.

Fiery Arrows → Intense Spiritual Warfare

"The shield of faith, with which you can extinguish all the flaming darts of the evil one." (Ephesians 6:16 NKJV)

If you dream of flaming arrows, it may mean you are under strong demonic attack, requiring urgent prayer and fasting.

Bow and Arrows → Divine Strategy, Warfare in Prayer

"Your arrows are sharp in the heart of the king's enemies."
(Psalm 45:5)

A bow with arrows may indicate God giving you strategic insight and intercessory power.

How to Respond to Weapon Dreams

Step 1: Identify Who Holds the Weapon

- Is it you? (God is empowering you for spiritual warfare.)
- Is it an enemy? (You are under attack and need to pray for protection.)
- Is it an angel? (Divine assistance is being sent to help you.)

Step 2: Determine the Purpose of the Weapon

- Offensive (sword, arrows, spears) ➙ God may be calling you to action, prayer, or intercession.
- Defensive (shield, armor) ➙ You may need to strengthen your faith and resist spiritual attacks.

Step 3: Pray for Discernment and Protection

- Ask God for revelation—what is this dream warning or preparing you for?
- Cover yourself in prayer, rebuke demonic attacks, and declare God's protection.

Final Thoughts on Weapons in Dreams

Weapons symbolize spiritual battles, divine empowerment, and protection.

- Recognize the weapons God has given you.
- Use the Word of God as your sword against the enemy.
- Pray and take authority over any demonic attacks revealed in your dreams.

Are you using the spiritual weapons God has given you?

9. Doors and Gates in Dreams

Doors and gates in dreams symbolize opportunities, transitions, spiritual access, or divine authority. They often represent the choices we face, the paths available to us, or the barriers that may stand in our way. Throughout Scripture, doors and gates are significant spiritual symbols, often used to describe:

- Opportunities and divine openings (Revelation 3:8).
- Access to God's kingdom and spiritual realms (Matthew 16:19).
- Closed or locked doors representing hindrances or seasons of waiting (Isaiah 22:22).
- Revolving doors symbolizing cycles and repeated experiences.

When interpreting a dream about doors or gates, consider:

- Is the door open, closed, locked, or revolving?
- Where does the door lead (a house, a church, a city, the unknown)?
- Are you passing through the door or struggling to enter?
- What emotions do you feel in the dream— excitement, fear, confusion, peace?

This section explores common door and gate symbols in dreams, their biblical significance, and how to interpret and respond to them.

An Open Door → A New Opportunity or Calling

An open door in a dream often represents a new season, divine opportunity, or answered prayer. Jesus says in Revelation 3:8 NKJV:

"See, I have set before you an open door that no one can shut."

An open door in a dream may indicate:

- A divine invitation into a new calling, ministry, or job.
- God providing an opportunity that cannot be stopped by man.
- A breakthrough after a season of waiting.
- Entering into a deeper relationship with God.

Example Dream Interpretation

- If you dream of walking through an open door into a bright place, it may symbolize stepping into a season of divine favor and new beginnings.
- If an angel stands by an open door, it may mean God is leading you into a spiritual awakening or deeper calling.
- If you see multiple open doors, it may indicate many choices and a need for discernment.

Your Response: Pray for wisdom and clarity about the opportunity ahead, and step forward in faith.

A Locked or Closed Door → Hindrances, Waiting Seasons

A locked or closed door can symbolize barriers, delays, or a waiting period before a breakthrough. Isaiah 22:22 NKJV declares:

"What He opens, no one can shut, and what He shuts, no one can open."

A locked or closed door in a dream may indicate:

- A spiritual or physical hindrance delaying progress.
- A season where patience and trust in God's timing are required.
- God preventing you from stepping into something that is not His will.
- A need to seek prayer and breakthrough for obstacles in your life.

Example Dream Interpretation

- If you struggle to open a locked door, it may symbolize an opportunity you desire but is not yet available.
- If you knock on a door, but no one answers, it could indicate a time of waiting or the need for persistence in prayer.
- If a door closes in your face, it may mean God is redirecting you away from something not meant for you.

Your Response: Ask God if He wants you to persist in prayer or if He is leading you toward a different path.

A Revolving Door → Cycles, Repeating Patterns

A revolving door can symbolize a cycle that keeps repeating —either a lesson that hasn't been learned or a spiritual stronghold that needs breaking. Ecclesiastes 1:9 NKJV says:

"What has been will be again, what has been done will be done again; there is nothing new under the sun."

A revolving door in a dream may indicate:

- Being stuck in repetitive cycles—spiritual stagnation or bad habits.
- Going in circles instead of progressing forward.
- A pattern of making the same mistakes or struggling with the same issues.
- A call to break free from destructive cycles and embrace transformation.

Example Dream Interpretation

- If you dream of walking through a revolving door but ending up where you started, it may symbolize frustration and a lack of progress in an area of your life.
- If you keep entering and exiting the same door, it may indicate double-mindedness or indecision (James 1:8).
- If someone pulls you out of the revolving door, it may represent divine intervention breaking a cycle in your life.

Your Response: Ask God to reveal if there is a cycle that needs breaking and seek deliverance and direction.

A Gate → Authority, Access to Spiritual Realms

A gate in a dream represents spiritual authority, access to divine realms, or transitions between natural and supernatural dimensions. Jesus said in Matthew 16:19 NKJV:

"I will give you the keys of the kingdom of heaven; whatever you

bind on earth will be bound in heaven, and whatever you loose on earth will be loosed in heaven."

A gate in a dream may indicate:

- God granting you greater spiritual authority.
- Access to new levels of revelation and anointing.
- A transition into a deeper spiritual walk.
- An entrance into God's promises or supernatural experiences.

Example Dream Interpretation

- If you walk through a golden gate, it may symbolize entering into divine favor or heavenly encounters.
- If a gate is guarded by angels, it may indicate a sacred place that requires spiritual readiness to enter.
- If a gate is locked, it could mean spiritual access is being restricted due to disobedience or lack of preparation.

Your Response: Seek deeper intimacy with God and pray for spiritual access and greater authority.

Other Door and Gate Symbols in Dreams

A Door Slamming Shut → God Closing a Chapter

If a door slams shut in a dream, it may indicate:

- God is closing a chapter in your life and leading you elsewhere.

- A situation that seemed promising is no longer part of your path.

Holding a Key → Authority to Unlock Something

If you hold a key in a dream, it may symbolize:

- God granting you access to a new opportunity or revelation.
- Spiritual authority over a situation or person.

"I will place on his shoulder the key to the house of David; what he opens no one can shut, and what he shuts no one can open."
(*Isaiah 22:22 NKJV*)

A Door Leading to Darkness → Spiritual Danger

If you see a door leading to a dark or unknown place, it may indicate:

- Entering something that is spiritually harmful or deceptive.
- A warning to avoid certain choices, relationships, or activities.

Large Gates Leading to a City → Influence, Leadership

If you walk through massive gates into a city, it may symbolize:

- God granting you influence in ministry, business, or leadership.

- A calling to impact nations and large groups of people.

How to Interpret and Respond to Door and Gate Dreams

Step 1: Identify the Condition of the Door or Gate

- Is it open, closed, locked, broken, or revolving?
- Does it lead to something good or dangerous?

Step 2: Pay Attention to Your Actions

- Are you walking through, knocking, struggling, or turning back?
- Are you holding keys, trying to open a door, or hesitating?

Step 3: Seek God's Direction

- Is this dream revealing an opportunity, transition, or warning?
- Is God opening or closing something in your life?

Final Thoughts on Doors and Gates in Dreams

Doors and gates represent transitions, opportunities, and spiritual authority.

- Pray for wisdom to discern open and closed doors.
- Trust God's timing—what He opens, no one can shut.

- Walk through the doors He provides with faith and boldness.

What doors is God opening or closing in your life?

10. People in Dreams: Understanding Their Spiritual Significance

People in dreams can carry deep symbolic meanings and often represent:

- Yourself (literal meaning).
- A characteristic or spiritual influence (positive or negative).
- A specific role, calling, or ministry.

Throughout Scripture, God used people in dreams to reveal divine messages, callings, and warnings:

- Joseph's dream of his brothers bowing before him revealed his future leadership (Genesis 37:5-11).
- Pharaoh's dream of seven fat and seven thin cows was interpreted by Joseph as a prophecy of famine (Genesis 41:1-32).
- Pilate's wife was warned in a dream about Jesus' innocence (Matthew 27:19).

Key Considerations When Interpreting People in Dreams:

- Is the person someone you know or a stranger?
- What is the person doing in the dream?
- Does the person remind you of someone else in your life?

- What emotions do you feel toward the person in the dream?

This section explores the common meanings of people in dreams, their biblical significance, and how to interpret them wisely.

<u>People Representing Themselves (Literal Meaning)</u>

Sometimes, the people in your dream are exactly who they appear to be. If you dream about:

- A family member, friend, or acquaintance, the dream may be directly related to that person.
- A coworker or pastor, the dream may involve your workplace or church.
- Yourself, the dream may reveal insights about your spiritual condition, emotions, or struggles.

Example Dream Interpretation

- If you dream of a close friend, it may indicate something significant happening in their life that requires your attention or prayer.
- If you see yourself struggling in a dream, it may represent an internal battle you are currently facing.
- If you argue with a family member in a dream, it could reflect unresolved issues that need addressing in real life.

Your Response: Pray for clarity—if the dream concerns someone specific, ask God if you should intercede for them, reach out to them, or pay attention to a particular situation in their life.

<u>People Representing a Characteristic or Spiritual Influence</u>

Many times, people in dreams are not literal but symbolic, representing a spiritual force, personality trait, or influence in your life. For example:

- A kind and wise old man may represent wisdom, guidance, or the Holy Spirit leading you.
- A police officer may symbolize God's protection, correction, or the presence of spiritual authority.
- A beggar may represent humility, neediness, or a call to generosity.
- A woman dressed in white may symbolize purity, righteousness, or an angelic presence.

Example Dream Interpretation

- If you dream of a tall, imposing figure blocking your path, it could represent a spiritual hindrance, fear, or demonic opposition.
- If you see a child playing joyfully, it may symbolize innocence, renewal, or a return to childlike faith.
- If you meet a stranger who gives you a message, it may be a divine revelation or an angelic encounter.

Your Response: Ask God if the person in your dream represents a spiritual influence—whether positive or negative—and seek His guidance on how to respond.

<u>People Representing a Role or Calling</u>

Certain figures in dreams may symbolize your calling, leadership, or a specific ministry assignment. For example:

- A pastor in a dream may represent spiritual leadership, guidance, or authority in your life.
- A teacher may symbolize a calling to instruct others in the Word of God.
- A prophet in a dream may indicate a season of spiritual growth, prophetic insight, or a divine message being given to you.

Example Dream Interpretation

- If you dream of your pastor praying for you, it may indicate a season of spiritual covering or mentorship needed in your life.
- If you see yourself preaching to a crowd, it may symbolize God calling you into a teaching or leadership role.
- If a prophet or biblical figure appears to you in a dream, it may be a direct message from God concerning your calling.

Your Response: Ask God if He is revealing a calling or preparing you for a leadership role in your faith journey.

Common People and Their Symbolic Meanings in Dreams

Father Figure → God the Father, Spiritual Authority

"I will be a Father to you, and you shall be My sons and daughters, says the Lord Almighty." (2 Corinthians 6:18 NKJV)

A loving father in a dream may symbolize:

- God's protection, provision, and love.
- A call to submit to spiritual authority.

An abusive or absent father in a dream may indicate:

- A struggle with trust in God.
- A need for healing from past wounds.

Mother Figure → Nurturing, Church, Holy Spirit

"As a mother comforts her child, so will I comfort you." (*Isaiah 66:13 NKJV*)

A mother in a dream may symbolize:

- Comfort, wisdom, and spiritual nurturing.
- The role of the Church as a place of growth and support.

A controlling or angry mother may indicate:

- Feeling smothered or restricted in your spiritual journey.

Child → Innocence, New Beginnings, or Immaturity

"Whoever humbles himself like this child is the greatest in the kingdom of heaven." (*Matthew 18:4 NKJV*)

A joyful child may represent:

- Spiritual renewal, faith, and innocence.
- God birthing something new in your life.

A lost or crying child may indicate:

- Emotional wounds, unresolved trauma, or feeling spiritually lost.

Stranger → Angelic Messenger or Unknown Spiritual Influence

> *"Do not forget to show hospitality to strangers, for by doing so some people have entertained angels without knowing it."*
> *(Hebrews 13:2 NKJV)*

A stranger offering guidance may symbolize:

- An angelic encounter or divine message.
- A call to embrace an unexpected spiritual lesson.

A threatening stranger may represent:

- A demonic presence or spiritual attack.
- Fear of the unknown or hidden dangers.

Crowd of People → Influence, Community, or Confusion

> *"A city set on a hill cannot be hidden."* (Matthew 5:14 NKJV)

A friendly crowd may symbolize:

- Influence and leadership over a group.

- A call to evangelism or ministry.

A chaotic or angry crowd may indicate:

- Spiritual distraction, confusion, or feeling overwhelmed.

How to Discern Whether a Person in a Dream Is Literal or Symbolic

Step 1: Pray for Discernment

- Ask God, "Is this person literal, or do they represent something greater?"

Step 2: Analyze the Dream Context

- What is the person doing?
- Do they resemble someone you know or a biblical figure?
- Is their presence positive or negative?

Step 3: Compare With Scripture

- Does the dream align with biblical patterns?
- Does the person's role match biblical symbolism?

Step 4: Seek Confirmation

- If the dream feels significant, ask for confirmation through prayer, Scripture, or wise counsel.

Final Thoughts on People in Dreams

People in dreams often carry profound meanings—whether they represent themselves, a spiritual influence, or a divine calling.

- Pay attention to their actions, words, and roles in the dream.
- Ask the Holy Spirit for wisdom to discern literal versus symbolic meaning.
- Pray for revelation about any message, warning, or encouragement God is communicating.

Who has appeared in your dreams lately, and what might God be saying through them?

How to Use This Dream Dictionary

1. Pray for Discernment

The Holy Spirit is the ultimate interpreter of dreams. Ask for revelation and clarity before applying any symbolic meanings.

"However, when He, the Spirit of truth, has come, He will guide you into all truth..." (John 16:13 NKJV)

2. Consider Context and Personal Meaning

Not all symbols mean the same thing for everyone. A dog in a dream may represent loyalty to one person and a negative experience to another. Make sure to look at the entire dream and how you felt in it.

3. Compare With Scripture

Dreams should align with biblical truth. If an interpretation contradicts God's Word, it is incorrect. Use the Bible as your primary source for interpretation.

4. Seek Confirmation

If a dream is prophetic or directional, seek wise counsel before acting on it (Proverbs 11:14 NKJV).

About the Author

Tom Cornell is the Senior Leader of SOZO Church in Washington state, founder of Walk in the Light International and SOZO Network. Tom is married to his beautiful wife Katy and lives in the Puget Sound area with her and their three kids. He has been in ministry pastoring and teaching the body of Christ since 2008.

He has a passion to see the body of Christ moving from people with an orphan mindset to that of sonship; equipping the body to do the work of Jesus resulting in seeing the Kingdom of God manifested here on earth.